FREEDOM(E) BY

Melody, thank you
Tell me what you think of it. Reach out
to me, you can find me on facebook. One love.

(Knowledge)

FREEDOM(E)

FREEDOM(E)

A NOVEL

BY

JASON MCMILLAN

FREEDOM(E)

Master Publisher: Remember To ThinkPink Publications©. Dallas, Texas.

DEDICATION

This book is dedicated to my Grandparents Nalder Taylor and Elizabeth Hicks.

To my special brother Devante Mulder-Grant who always asks the right question. To my Parents the best two parents one could ask for. To a longtime friend who sadly is currently locked down in prison. A special dedication to my Goddaughter Naomi, may you live long and prosper. To my Brothers, Sisters, and my Great-Great-Great Aunt Burnnet "Bunnie" Taylor, my "Double-G Aunt" I AM with you. I love you!

A very special dedication to our Nobel Peace Prize Winner Stanley "Tookie' Williams.

And finally, another special thank you to my Parents who have always pushed me forward on life's journey.

One!

~ Jason M.

FREEDOM(E)

INTRODUCTION

FreeDom-(e):

FreeDom(e): Freedom from negative cyclical strongholds. Freedom to identify such cycles destroy and rebuke them. Something must take its place.

Create a new, better, greater more holistically beneficial something-to-fill-the-void.

This is the chamber (situation) I'm working through now. What started as just few minutes a day was cultivated into much more.

Believing in yourself, a relationship with the most-high, and pure intent are tools for freedom. We must each take our own path to grab hold of mental, physical and spiritual freedom in relation to the world we live in today.

CHAPTER O

THE VOICE

I should have listened. I should have listened to the small voice of God while in my bedroom. The voice that told me to leave my gun where it was. I rebelliously took the gun anyway, thinking it was better to be a suspect than a victim. Shortly after leaving, I was pulled over by the police.

Have you ever thought to yourself you'd thought you would had learned already? That's how I felt. So, when the laws flipped on their lights, I had to think quickly. Police are known for killing unarmed black men, so I didn't want to give them any reason to be threatened by my actions. Even when they pleasantly ask you to step out of the car and put your hands behind your back, some police just violently take black men to the ground with no probable cause, other than racial profiling, while saying stop resisting.

I decided to take my chances and make a run for it. I put my foot down and the v8 under the hood picked up in response. I had to ease up on the gas and slow the vehicle because my left turn was coming up and I couldn't afford to lose control of the car. I ran a red light and barely made it through the light when a car nearly crashed into the left side of my rear end. My left turn must've been nice for me to escape that accident, especially having picked up some speed.

I got a hundred feet or so up the block when I looked in my rear-view mirror and saw the police car making the

FREEDOM(E)

turn and crossing the intersection I had just crossed a few short seconds ago. I made another left turn and eased off the gas pedal because I knew too much power and speed could easily transform a turn into tragic accident. An accident I could not afford right now.

The left turn led me to a dead end with the police, or "The Boys" as we call them, behind and closing in. My thoughts were focused on the fact that I knew I couldn't get stopped and searched with the gun on me! Seriously! If they stopped me, search me and found the gun things will not be good for me. I knew that if they did any forensics on the weapon they would match it to the shooting that occurred the past week. The shooting which happened just around the corner from this dead end I was approaching. Had I stopped when the police's siren had signaled me, they would have stopped me on the same corner of the shooting with the same gun that was involved. The more I thought about I, the more I realized that stopping was not an option, at least not until I had gotten enough distance between them and I to unnoticeably throw away my gun.

Several police cars pull behind me in the dead end. It was the end of the line for my whip, but not for me. I placed my left foot out of the car door and begin to exit my car as if nothing had happened. I was shocked to notice law boys behind me. Because I hadn't stopped when and where they signaled, they were pissed. The trooper exited his car matching the speed of me exiting mine. When he saw me get out and place a foot on the ground, he stopped in his tracks and pointed for me to get back into the car. I knew that this was my chance to run on foot. Damn! I realized the car didn't go into the

PARKED gear fully so my time to make a calculated escape and get some foot distance between us was slowly leaving, just like my car.

I could feel the car moving forward slowly. My right foot was still in the car and hadn't touched the ground yet, so I got back in the car to place it in park. The trooper probably thought I was complying with his hand signal to get back in the car. Wrong! As soon as I got the car into park I shot out of the already open driver door and was going…going…gone!

I had only taken a few steps when I heard the law boy yell out "stop or I'll taze you!" To me it sounded more like if I stop I *will* be tazed. It's no secret. We all know the police kill unarmed black men, young black boys, even our black woman for simple traffic stops, so do you think it was hard for me to dip on them? Not at all. There was no way he was going to get a chance to taze me unless he could grow wings and fly.

I took four long strides and I was out of sight and around the first corner that came up to my left. Sprinted a few more yards and took another left at the corner. I realized now that no one was at my heels, this would probably be the only chance I'd get to throw away my gun. I knew I wanted it back after all this, so I made sure to pay attention to where I tossed it. I spotted a square-shaped bush that looked different from the others that were clustered together, so I decided to toss the gun there. I made another few corners and was glad I was a safe distance from the cops. I was also relieved that I no longer had the gun on my waist. I was still hot about them profiling me in the first place.

FREEDOM(E)

I was on the sidewalk with my hands clasped together behind my head. Part of me wanted to go back to the scene where officers were probably searching my car and conjuring up a story. I was going to freestyle this story about being at a party and having my car stolen after I passed out drunk, but as I was contemplating my lie, a white Dodge Intrepid came up the street and two women waved for me to jump in their car. They instructed me to lay my head down so no passing cars would notice a third person in the car. Just in time! it was my "Triple OG's" wife and her girlfriend. They told me they were driving and saw the whole thing unfold and followed behind at a safe distance. I thanked them, and I thanked Jah, Allah, God looking out for me. I was grateful. I was grateful these women had kept their eyes on me.

From the floor of the car I could look at the power lines and the telephone poles and see we were headed back to where my big homie lived with his wife and family. I was correct. We pulled into the drive way and I jumped out of the car and rushed inside. Que, who was my homeboy Jeffrey's wife, walked into the house quickly yelling for "JDub" (Jeffreys' nickname) to come into the living room. When he saw me, he asked what was up? His wife quickly told him what had just happened. He was in just as much shock as the three of us were. He wanted to know from me personally the deal on what had happened. I told him how I was at the store getting money out of the ATM when I had come out of the store and seen our homeboy James in the parking lot. I explained to "JDub" how me and James were just standing in the parking lot talking. Him sitting in his car, me standing next to mine, when a Trooper passed by and nearly broke his neck looking at us. The trooper must have circled the block because as soon as I had pulled out of the store's parking lot, that same trooper was headed in my direction and then pulled a U turn a few cars behind me signaling for me to stop. I recounted how I just kept on going, came to a dead end and got out running!

"Man, that's wild!" "JDub" said in amazement. He told me how glad he was that his wife and her friend were there and could help. I told him that I was the one who was happy! I was safe with good friends and home-free. This night I would not be questioned by the profiling trooper or drug, tazed, or shot by them either.

I began being bombarded by overwhelming thoughts. I inhaled deeply through my nose. My car, I loved that car. The way a man loves a car. I hoped no one noticed me toss the burner in the bush and let the police know.

My job. My sister had gotten my foot in the door with this job now it was going to look as after one day I had had enough of it which was not the case.

I could just imagine me calling in saying "Hello...Yes...its Jason. I can't come in ever because I'm on the run from the police and they are going to be looking for me."

I knew they never got a look at my face, but the car was registered in my name, so although they would know I was the owner of the vehicle, they couldn't prove that I was the one driving that night. Exhale.

I finally stopped pacing and had a seat at the dining room table. I knew I was at home away from home.

FREEDOM(E)

"JDub's" home was a beautiful two-story that ducked off on our north side just out the blue. Lots of square footage and expensive furniture made his home a real playa pad. He and his wife had six children with three that still lived at home with them. It was normal for me to be there on any given day. "JDub" let me know that he was glad the police didn't get me, and I was welcome to stay long as I wanted.

This was around the end of the year and I had to also consider some other things. Things like I didn't want to be locked down in some brick mansion left with four walls to look at! Especially since this was the time of year my family starts to meet at my Mom's, Aunt's, or other relatives' homes. Family will just start showing up for the holidays. So, I

I was glad to have another day in paradise. My current situation was better than ten minutes before! I was still trying to calm myself by simply not stressing and letting go getting over negative thoughts. Realizing it would be worse if they had caught me!

CHAPTER ONE

THIRTIES & 40'S

"JDub" interrupted my thoughts by asking me if I wanted some of his forty. I told him that I needed my own and pulled out enough cash so that we could each have two forties a piece.

"JDub" and Que said they'd stop by the store on the way back from picking up their kids.

The rest of the evening wasn't so bad after everyone returned home. The children put a smile on my face. I was like a big brother to them. We played and argued just like normal siblings. After roughhousing with the kids, I needed a drink and some smoke.

Que and I smoked a blunt while "JDub" and I drank our forties. He had a banging stereo sound system in his house, so we listened to music and as always, had a good time, especially compared to earlier when I nearly got jammed up with that pistol.

The kids had long since fallen asleep and us adults had been up drinking, smoking, and jamming. We were all exhausted after the day we had so we called it a night. I slept on "JDub's" couch that night and would be there for the next three months.

We had a regular routine. Que would get the kids ready for school and then go to her client's home where she

FREEDOM(E)

worked as a nurse's aide. "JDub" only worked three days out of the week, so he and I mostly stayed at the house. Music always played in the background at his place. It was a nice atmosphere. He told me I could stay with them for as long as I wanted to. He meant it too! Part of me had always just wanted to be free and on my own. Don't get me wrong I could have walked out the door at any time, but I didn't want any more altercations with the police.

Although I walked around freely, I still looked over my shoulder, ready to blaze at the slightest sign of police. It wasn't easy feeling like you must look over your shoulder. I knew that if I saw them I would have to remain calm and remember that they never actually saw my face, so it wasn't like my picture was plastered on the news, but just to be safe, I kept my eyes open for undercover detective cars.

After a few days I began to feel lighter. I was beginning to come to terms with the fact that the police would eventually catch up with me. It would be sometime after I decide to come up from the "underground", so I was happy knowing it wasn't going to happen in the blink of an eye like it almost did the last time. I was going to have to turn myself in or something like that. I was using this time to get mentally prepared for the possibility that I may be soon locked up. I was free but still "confined" at "JDub's" house. I had freedom(e) to think before being cuffed and transported. Held against my will. I made a conscious decision to run for my life, knowing how things could have gone had the laws gotten their hands on me. I was thankful that I was at "JDub's" house and not in a cell block. It wasn't bad at all at "JDub's", I did my part around the house to make sure I didn't wear out my welcome. I would wash the dishes and take out the trash. They had taken me in on a moment's notice with nothing to contribute to the bills, so it was only right that I did my part by helping around the house. I made sure they would never feel as if I was just a freeloader taking advantage.

The days were long and beautiful, and the evenings short and sweet. This was the longest time I'd ever stayed with "JDub" and his family. I think "JDub" and Que may have been some of the most down to earth parents I have ever met.

For example, "JDub" would rather you smoke cannabis in his home than tobacco cigarettes because of all the additives and negative effects of tobacco. I admired his outlook on this because I know people who smoke cannabis and cigarettes, like myself. Smoking cigarettes publicly was socially acceptable although second-hand smoke warnings were becoming a pressing issue. However, if I were to light a joint or a blunt in public some people would look at me like "Is he smoking weed?" and call the law. I think it should be the other way around, I think we should say nothing about a person that chooses to smoke cannabis in public or in the comfort of their own home or whatever, and we the masses should frown upon those who smoke tobacco in public or around others especially children.

Shit they say second hand smoke is and can be worse than first hand. If that's the case someone who is close by another who smokes habitually may as well just start first hand smoking. That shouldn't be the case, but I'm just making a point.

FREEDOM(E)

The family makes me feel right at home. I had a plate
and a seat at the table every dinner. I had everything I
needed. Hygiene, tooth brush, wash cloth and towel.
They never made me feel I was out of place. I could
help myself to breakfast or anything in the fridge even
if no one else was there.

After a few weeks my money was running low. I had
given "JDub" seventy dollars when I first started
staying over at their place. I knew it wasn't much, but I
also knew he understood my situation and was thankful
I had given something. Not to mention, I had been
rotating the same clothes. I decided to go home to my
apartment just to grab a few things. I knew I couldn't
stay long because the block would be hot considering
all recent activity. There was the chase between me and
the police, the shooting a few days before that as well
as normal hood activity.

I laced up my shoes and did a quick visual scan of all
the back-alley routes and short cut getaways then
headed out. I needed to identify all my points of getaway. The key to walking free while on "the run" is
having the ability of being able not to panic every time
you see or come across a law boy. I hadn't killed
anyone, so I knew they may only have had a few
detectives on the case. Even though I was sure they
mentioned the chase and abandoned car every morning
during shift change before the officers went on duty and
out into the streets. I laughed out loud imagining the
officers showing my picture on a big screen. If they saw
me they'd probably be too embarrassed to stop me,
considering the state trooper let me get away in a foot
chase.

I walked down the street as if nothing had ever happened. My thoughts, on the other hand, were focused on keeping the getaway routes fresh in my mind and going over them silently as I moved throughout the path from "JDub's" house to my apartment. As I approached the corner and made a right turn, I assured myself that it wasn't that bad. It wasn't like I was on America's Most Wanted or something.

As I continued down the hill of Fourth Street my feet couldn't help but to pick up the pace as the steepened. I smiled knowing that this was one of the steepest hills in our town. Towards the bottom of the hill I realized I had many routes to choose from. I stayed low-key and took the alley behind the dollar store at the corner of fourth and Market Street.

This was my usual route anyway, so nothing out of the normal for anyone who may have noticed me. I approached what was literally an alley. You could drive a car through it, and people did sometimes. The privacy fences of backyards, trees, and homes on both sides of the ally made them perfect for times such as this one.

When I reached the end of the street, I turned to the left, waited for a break in the cars going up and down-market street, and then crossed. As I headed down the street, I see the building located directly behind my building and walked through the parking lot. As I came out the other side of the building and reach the back door of my apartment complex, I reached for my keys. I needed to have them ready to make a quick entrance into my apartment.

FREEDOM(E)

It felt awkward to have to use alternate routes to get home. Usually if an alternate route was used it would be a group of the us at a spot that would get hot. We'd each dash off in alternate directions and each of us would take a different path to their respective houses.

I entered the building and into my apartment. When I unlocked the door, I was startled at my Father standing in the living room. My sister and I shared the apartment, so I wasn't surprised that someone was there, I just didn't expect him to be there repairing the front door.

I flashed my Dad a big smile. I admired him and whenever I saw him I felt loved. It had been a while since I saw him. He walked towards me, greeting me warmly, and embracing me in a hug. I couldn't help but to feel somewhat down because I knew that if my Father knew about the current and previous string of bad events, he'd be very disappointed in me.

"I wasn't expecting to see you here," My Father said with a smile.

I wasn't sure if he was being sarcastic, already knowing what had transpired, or if he was genuinely happy to see me. I decided to bank on the latter. To be able to lay eyes on my Father whom I hadn't seen in five years was already emotional. I shook my head slightly and smiled brightly at my Father. It had slipped my mind that this was the month he was supposed to be moving in to live with us for good! I was ashamed for forgetting. I asked him what he was doing to the front door and where was my sister Diana.

My Dad explained that he was working on the threshold of the front door and told me that my sister was gone to work. I let him know where I would be staying for about a month. I told him that I had only come back to grab some clothing and hygiene to last me.

Still wearing a smile as if I could do nothing wrong in his eyes, my Father said okay and that he was finished and leaving but would soon be back to move in with us. We hugged again, and I watched him go down the street.

I went into my bedroom and grabbed my backpack to fill it with clothes and whatever else I could think of to bring that I might need. I pulled open my drawers, pulling out clothes, then placing them neatly into the backpack. I looked around the room realizing I may not be returning for a while. I left my room to go to my stash spot I had in the apartment. I opened the stash jar to see it just as I left it.

An airtight jar with some sticky green cannabis inside. I placed the jar into my bag and gave the apartment one last look to see if there was anything else I needed. "There was nothing I need besides my life back!" I thought to myself and almost laughed out loud.

Looking out of the window through the blinds to make sure the coast was clear, and the police were not outside ready to bag me, I took a deep breath and walked through the threshold of the apartment to face the world, locking the door behind me.

As soon as I stepped outside I remembered the gun I'd thrown the night the police had me surrounded. The bush where I stashed the gun was just around a couple

FREEDOM(E)

of corners. I walked in that direction to see if I could find it. As I arrived at the house where the bush was, I knew I had to be quiet and get in and out of the yard without being noticed.

I turned the corner and see the bush. I noticed that the bush had a slim trunk and didn't go all the way to the ground. It wasn't the full- type bush like I thought at first. Surprisingly, the gun was laying there for anyone to see, next to the skinny trunk of the bush.

"Wow!" I thought to myself, "I'm glad I had a few corners distance between us or they would have had no problem finding it!"

I reached down quickly to pick it up and place it into my waist line. I didn't see anyone, so I ran back to my apartment to stash it there. There was no way I would bring a gun to "JDub's" house because I respected his wife and children. After I put the gun in a safe place, I moved swiftly through the streets headed back to "JDub's" place. Upon returning to "JDub's", I unloaded my backpack, placing my clothes and things into a small closet where my covers and pillow were already being kept.

I thought back on the incident that caused me to be sleeping on "JDub's" couch. I couldn't help but think back to what all went wrong that day. Before anything had transpired I believe they'd racially profiled me while I was just standing in front of the store being black. Damn!

I tried to shake off all my thoughts about that day and set about making plans for my immediate future. I had given "JDub" some money the last month, not much just something to show him I knew that nothing came free, but I had no more money now and the end of the year was coming fast. Time waits on no one! I had thought to call my Mother and ask her to borrow some money, so I could give "JDub" some money for this month, anything. Even though he wasn't asking I knew it was the best thing to do.

So, I called. I dialed the number the telephone began to ring.

A sweet voice answered "Hello."

"Hello Mother" I replied. I immediately let her know I was safe and alright. I explained to her my situation I told her how I felt about everything "JDub" and his family has done for me. I was only asking if I could borrow some money to give them something.

She hesitated for a brief second. Then she asked me "Jason what are you going to do when this money runs out?"

I thought for a second and told my mom the truth. That I was on the run, but I didn't plan on being on the run for long, just till after the new year. Her question did cause me to reevaluate my life. Is this the way I wanted to spend the rest of my life? Ducking, dodging, and committing crimes? I knew my Mother and Father loved me and would always love me.

I seemed to always get in trouble every time I turned around. Even if I wasn't getting in trouble, I wasn't doing anything productive.

If I worked, I never saved or put any money to the side. If I had, I would have been able to jump on a profitable

FREEDOM(E)

opportunity if one would have come my way . I didn't want to die on the streets. I really wanted to make something of my life before my time on earth was over. I wanted to create something grand so that my parents could be proud. I couldn't help but to think how much I had let them down and disappointed them over the years.

After speaking with me, my Mother agreed to loan me some money. We agreed on the time and I told her I would meet her at her home. Just as I'd hung up, my brother Prince stopped by "JDub's" to visit. We all kicked it for a minute. I asked my brother if he wouldn't mind taking me to the spot to meet with moms. I didn't know what he had planned for the day and I hated to ask last minute, but he told me he was good with it and we jumped in his car to go meet our mom.

My mom's home wasn't far from "JDub's" house, so my brother and I bent a few corners, went down a few streets and we were there. I checked my surroundings just to make sure the police were nowhere around. They shouldn't be-there wasn't anything illegal going on at this house!

As I entered through the back door, my mom, who was cleaning, turned at the sound of the door closing behind me. Once she saw who I was, she flashed her brilliant smile. The smile I loved so much. I went to her and wrapped my arms around her. It felt good to feel her nurturing embrace as she rubbed and patted me on the back.

We sat and talked for a while. She wanted to share some important things she'd learned in life. One thing she told me was to always stay in the right frame of mind. When your mind is clear, your vision is clear, and you'll be able to spot amazing opportunities or stay away from the bad ones.

As I listened to my mother all I could think is that one day, I'm going to make my Mother and Father proud. I was also thinking how this was going to be my last time on the run. At this point, I didn't even want to get a traffic ticket.

Thinking about all this and the feeling of shame I had asking to borrow money from my Mom was depressing. The worst feeling is knowing I've let my Parents down.

After a few days with these thoughts, I did slip into depression. I had no appetite, so I lost weight. I also wanted to sleep all the time. I knew that these were symptoms of depression.

I remembered all the times I'd been doing good but here lately I hadn't been doing anything besides fucking around and doing things I had no business doing. Dwelling on thoughts like this made slip deeper into depression, and although it wasn't easy, I found myself having to redirect my thoughts several times a day. It was also depressing to know I wasn't at home, my home. Even though I was welcome at "JDub's" home, I missed the freedom of having my own space in the apartment I shared with my sister. I missed my car.

Speaking of my sister. I knew I'd let her down as well. She and I shared the apartment so that meant we shared the bills. Everything was going smooth until the one

FREEDOM(E)

day I didn't, couldn't come home. The rent, the water, the electricity; we split all the bills and I defaulted on my part because I had to get ghost on the state troopers. I knew she was disappointed as well as hot when she had to cover one hundred percent of the bills with such short notice.

I thought about my car. This really upset me because it was my first car AND my Mother helped me with some of the down payment as a birthday gift. The car meant a lot to me. I had always loved anything with wheels, so I was mad hurt about that. Even more hurt to know that the police had it. I found out later that it had been towed to the police impound.

CHAPTER TWO

THE MATRIX

My brother asked me to come to a show he was performing at. He didn't have to ask twice. I was there! He told our homeboys he'd take me to the spot to meet them, so I could ride with them into the next city where the performance was held.

That day was a normal day for the most part. We had a big breakfast, then I washed the dishes, turned on the stereo and smoked a blunt. Afterwards, I did my daily push-ups then chilled for the rest of the day. I was excited about going to support my brother that evening and I began getting ready. I took a nice long shower, put on fresh clothes, brushed my teeth and told "JDub" I was out.

I use the same allies and back roads to get into the hood. I needed to stop by my apartment to get some things I'd forgotten. As I walk to the front entrance, one of my female neighbors greets me warmly and goes into the building alongside me.

We each go into our own apartment and I gather a few things. A couple of pairs of shoes, a hat, and not too much else. I knew I couldn't stay inside the apartment long. As I looked around the apartment one last time, I

FREEDOM(E)

heard my neighbors through the wall. I was shocked after listening closely.

I heard her saying, "Did y'all catch him yet? Jason McMillan?"

I couldn't believe I blatantly heard her snitching on the telephone to whom I assumed was the police. I was pissed. I had never done anything but be nice and respectful to this lady. My being on the run had nothing to do with her and would not have affected her in anyway. She knew the case was blown out of proportion by the police. It hurt to know that she wanted to see me bagged by the police. I bugged out and jumped into high gear, grabbing my things and running out the back door.

I took a leap of faith and walked out as normally and as calmly as I could. I took an alternate route going through the south passage which ran parallel with the main Street.

I began walking towards my homeboy Vido's house who lived on the next block. It was the first safe house on this route. I knew I needed to get out of the streets quickly because the laws could turn the corner at any time, especially when they get the description of a Black male who coincidentally matches the Black male who recently evaded state troopers

I ran through the alley so that I could go through the threshold of the brick, bar-lighted fence surrounding his building. I flung open the door and ran up the flight of stairs to reach his apartment. When I arrived at the top of the stairs, I noticed his front door was open. Instead of barging in (even though I knew I was welcome) I knew I wouldn't want anyone walking into my apartment without being invited in. I yelled his name in a low, sharp voice and he emerged from the bedroom. As he walked through the corridor and saw me, he smiled.

"Come on in bro." He said to me ushering me inside, "What's good?"

What's good is that you let me in, I thought to myself, but despite being happy for his always open door, I couldn't help but think about my snitching neighbor.

I asked him to come to the window. It wasn't long before we saw the police pull up right in front of my building which was clearly visible from his upstairs apartment. There were at least 3 police cars with two police officers to a car. They rushed into my building like I was wanted for a mass murder spree.

We watched them surround the building. Little did they know I had heard my neighbor on the phone and was one step ahead of them. I was glad Vido's safe house was within a few minutes walking distance.

I shared with Vido how only a month before I had skated on the state troopers and was now on the run. I told him I regretted the incident, but he didn't hold it against me. He nodded and lit a smoke as I continued to tell him more. I explained how I'd been at "JDub's" up until this point but had went back to my apartment to retrieve some things before hitting my brother's show. I went on to tell him how my neighbor smiled and greeted me and then went right in her apartment and called the law. I felt betrayed because I knew I never had a problem

FREEDOM(E)

I told him how my neighbor has smiled in my face as if she had no problem with me and we greeted each other than both went inside. Then once inside I could hear her through the walls on the phone with the police giving them my name and telling them that I was in the building! I was still feeling betrayed. I had done nothing wrong to this lady. It would be another matter if I had done something wrong to her.

This incident with my snitching neighbor reminded me of the box office film, "The Matrix".

In this movie there was a character named Mr. Anderson. He was the agent whose tracked and destroyed those freed from the "Matrix". The matrix coincidentally was a world covered in deception. Sometimes when those freed from the matrix would be running from the agent Mr. Anderson and if anyone who was still a slave to the matrix would lay eyes on the freed soul whose eyes were open to the deception of the matrix, the person still enslaved would turn into Mar. Anderson which would duplicate the virus. My neighbor had shown me her true colors. She was easily overcome by the virus of deception.

Vido laughed as I told him my neighbor *was* Mr. Anderson! We shared a smoke and I checked the time. I knew I had to bounce so that I could be on time for my ride. I told him bye and waited on my brother to drop me off to the next city to meet up with the bros while he went ahead to prepare, and sound check his show.

I thanked him again as I braved the block and tried to avoid laws. Keeping my eyes open, I met my brother who raced off to the next city so that I could meet up with our homeboys. My head was on swivel as I reached the truck my homeboys were in.

I pulled the handle and it was locked, so I knocked on the window for someone to let me in. When I hear the power locks and see the door swing, I knew it was about to be on. We all greeted each other with a dap and asked each other what was up. Rob was driving, "D" was riding passenger, and I sat between Tommy and Brandon in the back.

As soon as he pulled off, Rob lit a blunt. We drove through the city towards the highway. Eventually it was my turn to pull from the trees. I inhaled and exhaled a deep breath before putting the blunt to my lips. Inhaling the smoke deeply and holding it for a whole minute cleared my head when I blew out the smoke.

I took my tokes and passed it on. It came back around in rotation and before we even finished smoking the first one, another was lit. We were rolling, jamming, and smoking down the highway on our way to hear my brother perform.

We drove down the street the night club was on, we noticed it up ahead on our left side. We kept driving past it because we knew you could smell the weed from our car. The police were outside the club with their lights flashing. We made sure all of us were cool and kept driving till we reached a convenient store. We sprayed the vehicle and bought some squares. By the time we make it back to the club, the police were gone, and we were once again ready to turn up.

We got to the club and the security guard mentioned that he saw us drive past. We explained that we were

FREEDOM(E)

blowing trees. We all laughed and dapped and went inside the club. I spotted my brother sitting at a table with a woman.

As soon as he saw me, he stepped up to me, gave me some dap, and a quick hug. He introduced me to the woman sitting at the table as Tasha. I spoke to her and she smiled at me warmly. She was cool. I liked her vibe. I told my brother to get on stage and do his thing. We dap again quickly before he rushed off backstage with the rest of the performers.

I sat down and the table with Tasha. She and I both sat in silence until they announced his name then I stood up screaming his name, hyping him up. Tasha gave me a look as if to say, 'Could you be any louder?' The twinkle in her eye let me know she was being humorous. I knew she wasn't embarrassed by me, she was probably just surprised how I went from the quiet little brother to his loudest hype man.

When my brother started to perform his select singles, I couldn't help but get louder. His first single of the night was "Tell Me What You Know About Snitches?" Since only an hour before I'd been snitched on, I felt him on this song. Everything he was been saying on stage was everything I had been going through as of late. The whole time he was on stage I was at the table with Tasha yelling at the top of my lungs agreeing, cosigning, and at the end of every bar, rapping along with him! Tasha ended up giving me several "You ratchet" looks a few times that night.

After the all the artist had performed, I could see my brother making his way back towards the table. Tasha and I were standing still hyped from the music the DJ was now playing. He and Tasha shared a few words and she gave him a sultry kiss. He walked my way after they have their moment. He chuckled when he saw me, talking about how I was hating. We both laughed and now that his show was finished, I caught him up on all the events that had taken place that day.

I stood where I'd been standing near the table as he and Tasha walk through the club making small talk with others. At one point I noticed them walking in front of the table again. Tasha leaned over and whispered something in his ear. My brother tilted his head down so that he could hear her over the music and nodded his head. From the look my brother shot me I figured maybe she was asking him if I could spend the night with them. It would be a break away from the city.

I was hoping she read my thoughts because I didn't want to go back to the city and must constantly look over my shoulder for the law.

My brother Prince walked towards me and I smiled in anticipation. I guess Tasha could feel my vibe or read my mind about wanting to stay.

When he reached me, he asked "Hey bro, who are you riding with when you leave here?"

This question was a subtle way of him letting me know I wasn't spending the night.

"I guess I'm going to ride with Rob, that's how I got here," I told him.

FREEDOM(E)

I looked at him a little sideways I did not believe that was the original message Tasha instructed him to send to me.

Somehow after the event was over with, I ended up being given a ride by my brother and his lady anyway. As we rode down the highway, passing the community college, and got closer to the city limits, my body started shaking. I was terrified at the thought of reentering the city limits. Tasha must have felt my knees trembling against her seat.

She turned around and said, "You know Jason any time you'd like you can come stay with us for a few nights if you'd like."

I exhaled a breath of relief. All the fear of being arrested was replaced by feelings of safety and comfort. It confirmed the feeling I had earlier that my brother disapproved, because as soon as she said it, he looked over and gave her a piercing glare.

Since I am never one to impose, I quickly mention that since we were so far along in the drive and closer to where I'd go than where they live, that they could just drop me off.

Even though she reassured me that I could come some other time, the fear returned, and I began to tremble again. As the flashing lights and neon signs became visible, I knew we were entering the city. I was shaking my head at the thought of being racially profiled and how the stigma of young, black men had been at the forefront of all the racial profiling, and the killing of young black males. All due to the labels that had been placed on us.

 She tells me some other time anytime, I am welcome to come visit. I tell her thank you and I mean it from the bottom of my heart. She tells me I am welcome in a sweet voice. During our words we had with each other I had stopped shaking. Now we had stopped talking and I had begun to tremble again as we get even closer to the city limits. Part of me wanted to ask them to just drop me off at the police department. I voiced this though out loud and my brother looked at me and told me I was tripping.

Damn. I knew eventually it was going to come down to dealing with this case and those prejudiced laws. The system wanted all Black males locked down. I compared the cell blocks in prison to "auction blocks" in slavery. I wanted to go on my own terms because I didn't want to be treated like a statistic. Just as I was about to ask my brother to stop at the upcoming police station, he zoomed past it like he knew what I was thinking.

I thanked them for the ride as we approached "JDub's" house. My brother told me to keep my head up and I assured him I would do my best. I knocked on the door three times. That was my knock to let them know it was me.

"JDub" opened the door and I walked in smelling the trees and noticed the drink in his hand. I knew I needed some trees to overcome tonight's events. Que was smoking a cigarette and pointed to the blunt in the ashtray. She told me that she saved it for me.

I light the blunt and inhale the smoke deeply. As I inhaled again, the smoke burned my lungs which

FREEDOM(E)

caused me to cough, which brought on my buzz. I passed the joint to Que and "JDub" asked me how the show was.

I told him what happened at the show and how dope it was but also mentioned my concern about my snitching neighbor. They shook their heads and wished me the best as we continued to smoke and zone.

CHAPTER THREE

LOVE WHILE UNDERGROUND

My family loved to throw dinner parties where different members just drop in to eat and fellowship. One of our famous family dinners was coming up in a few days. My brother and his woman, Tasha, had invited me to come and not only have dinner but to spend a few days with them. I accepted and was thankful. I had begun to feel more and more confined at "JDub's" home.

I packed a few things, a few clothes, my notebook and my blanket and was ready to roll. When I walked in the living room, I see my brother and "JDub" greeting each other with a dap. I told "JDub" that I was going to chill with my brother for a few days and give him some space to be with his family. He told me to stay safe, I assured him I would, then walked to my brother's car.

It took us 20 minutes from "JDub's" home to my brothers' apartment he shared with Tasha and their family. We didn't talk much during the ride, but I did tell him how grateful I was for the dinner invite and welcoming me to stay a few days. It felt good knowing I would be out of the city limits for a few days. It felt like a breath of fresh air!

We pulled into the parking lot and I flashed back to the fun memories I had spent in this very apartment building back in the day when I would kick it with my sister and her friends. One of her friends lived in this

FREEDOM(E)

very apartment complex, the other friend lived right across the street. Thoughts of BBQ's and the underage drinking and partying we all had done in the courtyard made me smile. There was never any harm done when we partied, just a lot of fun and cool times. They were all older than me, so it was always a good time hanging with them.

 I grabbed my bag and blanket from the back seat of the car and followed them into their apartment. When we entered I laid my eyes on the most precious little girl. She lowered her eyes shyly and attempted to hide her beautiful smile. As I tried to engage her in conversation, Tasha went to the kitchen preparing dinner. The food smelled delicious and my brother and Tasha kept making sure I was good.

I thought to myself, "What great hospitality from the people I have around me. This has been a time of struggle.

I considered this to be underground, mad love! I know I've been good to people because while underground the underground was good to me, in fact, great to me. I couldn't ask for any better treatment!

Shortly after dinner was ready we all sat at the table. Tasha said a prayer that was sweet and to the point and as we raised our heads, I couldn't help but to look upon every one of their faces knowing these are faces of true and unconditional love. They brought me into their home knowing I could not give them anything. There was no benefit to them from helping me! They gained nothing materialistically, they didn't ask for a room and board fee so, what was the purpose? They helped me, they supported me even if it was for just a few days, the impact of their unconditional love has me shedding even now as I realize the kindness and selflessness they displayed towards me.

The thought occurred to me that we all have problems of our own. Some may be hard for us to deal with and conquer on our own. These close friends, my extended family took me in while dealing with their own day to day and life situations. Knowing I had a problem, hell at the time I was a problem. A wanted man on the run from the state for a state felony!

After dinner, Tasha gathers the kids to put them to bed. My brother pulled out some bud a grinder and some Dutch's cigars, and begun the process of rolling up. It didn't take him long to roll the weed, then patiently waited while the children were tucked into bed, so Tasha can join us.

Realizing it may take a minute she yelled from the bedroom for us to go and get started without her. My brother and I made our way into the smoke spot of their apartment, which was their bathroom, so the smell wouldn't be all over the apartment and tenants couldn't get a whiff of it. We both sat on the edge of the tub while he lit the blunt. He takes his tokes and passes the leaf to me. While taking my tokes Tasha entered the bathroom and rolled her eyes as if the children were doing the most while being tucked in and we all laughed.

Tasha went on to describe how the kids were asking all these questions about me and it was hard to calm them down. We laughed again. When we finished smoking,

FREEDOM(E)

my brother let out the fold out couch letting me know that's where I'd be sleeping. We said goodnight and he went into the bedroom, ending the night, with Tasha.

The next morning, I awakened to realize everyone had already left the apartment. It was hard to believe everyone woke up and got ready for the day and I didn't hear a sound. I folded my sheets and covers and place the couch back to its normal position. Then reaching and grabbing my bag, I removed my shower things and my toothbrush. I took a shower, brushed my teeth, and cleaned the tub. I hoped Tasha and my brother would notice I was good at cleaning up behind myself as well as having good hygiene.

I walked through the living room to the kitchen and made myself a big bowl of cereal. After breakfast, I washed all the dishes in the sink. Not only were there dishes from their breakfast, there were dishes from last night's dinner as well. After I was through at the sink, I begun to wipe down all the counters, the stove top, and the outside of the refrigerator. This happened on every day I was stayed with them.

I didn't know how to work their television, so I decided to go for a walk through the neighborhood. I walked down to the park close by, taking my time not to rush my steps so that I could enjoy the breeze, the views of the rolling hills and the joy of still being free. I found a park table and sat on the bench for a while. Thinking, feeling. It was still good for me to get out of the city even if it was only the next city over.

After an hour and a half of walking, I begun to make my way back to the apartment, stopping at the corner store for a smoke. When I got back to the apartment, I sat down at their computer to surf the internet for more information on the Pinal gland, spelling it incorrectly I couldn't find much.

Later that afternoon when she and her daughter Nia returned, Tasha caught me off guard by asking me to stay with them for a few more days. My brother returned shortly after and all of us sat in comfort enjoying the evening.

My brother and I sat the table, Nia was in her room doing her homework, and Tasha was on the couch on her tablet. Tasha called my brother to look at something she'd found on the internet. She was looking at information on the pineal gland! Information I had been searching for earlier. This put a big smile on my heart. I thought to myself that she and I were connected mentally to have the same thoughts. I leaned over on my stool to see what information she had found. I was in awe. At once, I realized I had been spelling pineal incorrectly! I instantly admired the fact her and I had been having some of the same questions and searching for answers. What was not to love about her?!

 That evening dinner was lovely, even better than the last. Tasha prepared chicken and delicious sides. After we finished dinner my brother began to roll one up and we had a smoke session in the bathroom. After the session we all called it a night and went to bed resting for the next day.

The next morning, again, I woke up and everyone was gone. How could I not wake with people getting up showering and getting ready and hustling & bustling

FREEDOM(E)

out the door? I showered and dressed and made myself breakfast, and washed breakfast dishes and the dinner dishes from the night before.

As I did the day before, I took a walk around the huge neighborhood block. When I returned I saw a state trooper driving by and it made me nervous, but I kept walking as nonchalantly as I could. When I arrived at my bro's apartment he was sitting on the couch smoking a blunt, apparently having gotten off work early.

We sat and talked with each other and burned trees, the smoke giving us both a good buzz. Suddenly his phone rang, and it was a mutual friend of both ours. Our friend wanted to meet my brother to buy some trees from him. I didn't trust him. We called this dude "LDogg" because he was the type that would do anything for money. Even cross his so called "friends".

I had let my bro know the feelings that had come after I found out who he was on the phone with him. I suggested to my brother that he should meet him outside and not allow him inside of his house. My brother assured me he had served him before and he would always meet him outside. I also asked my brother not to say anything to him about me being there. He agreed, and I felt a little better.

Soon after his phone went off and it was LDogg letting him know he was outside. I had gotten up from my seat and took another seat because my previous seat put me in direct line to be seen through the door a window. I couldn't take any chances being caught and especially being caught at my brother's home where he and family lived. This could potentially give them a bad reputation also put them in jeopardy of them getting charged with harboring a fugitive.

My brother went outside and made the exchange. When he returned he had let me know my feelings were correct. He told me that L Dogg asked about me asking if he'd seen me lately. He also told me he kept peering in trying to get a sight of who was sitting on the other side of the door.

I didn't trust LDogg, not when it came to money or my freedom!

Tasha and Nia came home to find my brother and me discussing the LDogg situation. She walked into the living room and removed her shoes at the door. She stopped to give my brother a kiss and sent Nia to do her homework while she got dinner ready. Noticing the dishes were washed and the kitchen cleaned consecutively the past few days, she walked to my brother and wrapped her arms around his neck.

"Babe you cleaned the kitchen again?" She said smiling at him doing something he didn't usually do.

When my bro nodded his head yes, I was shocked! She stood on the tips of her toes and gave him another kiss and went happily to back to the kitchen to start dinner. Although I felt I shouldn't interfere with their relationship, I wanted to say something badly, but I was hoping my brother would eventually reveal the truth.

This night's dinner was the night of celebration and I felt like celebrating in my own special way. By living life to the fullest! My celebration was about life and

FREEDOM(E)

freedom(e). The dinner was especially good, and I asked if I could go back for seconds. I was told no, but I didn't mind. The question I asked was a yes or no question, so I was fine with being told no. Plus they had bills and of course a child to feed as well as themselves. The food was so good, and I was satisfied, but more would have only been a delight.

At that point, I knew it was time for me to say my goodbyes. Hugging Tasha and Nia tightly and telling them both how much I enjoyed them, I grabbed my belongings and got into the car with my brother. When we arrived at "JDub's" he greeted us both warmly and asked if we enjoyed our "brother" time together. Assuring him that we had, my brother headed out the door as I put my things away.

"JDub", as usual, had a drink and blunt for me. We smoked and sat in the living room. I looked over and let him know that I wouldn't be at his place much longer-two weeks at the most. It was time for our entire family to get together for the holidays and I needed to spend quality time with them.

The two weeks seemed to have flown by and I had already packed my things. I had phoned my parents earlier and they came to "JDub's" to pick me up and take me home with them.

Over the next few weeks I spent lots of quality time with my family. Being at my parents' house was truly a refuge. I spent the nights sitting with my family in the living room talking, watching movies, or playing cards. I felt free as if nothing had ever happened. I had no worries. We ate good, had lots of fun and even took a trip out of town to visit some extended family and close friends. Surrounded by family and all the genuine love I forgot my troubles. Being surrounded by my family I can honestly say again, this was mad underground because these people loved me unconditionally.

FREEDOM(E)

CHAPTER FOUR
TRICKERY

Shortly after the holiday celebrations had ended, I received a letter in the mail from the city court. I opened the letter to find a paper with a list of charges from the city. First was driving with no seat belt. Which was not true because I have always driven with a seat belt. I clearly remember removing my seat belt before I had exited the car to jet on foot.

I realized they were trumping up the charges They also charged me with possession of drug paraphernalia, and I knew this charge was trumped up as well. I'd always kept my car super clean, especially after an incident where my neighbor's girlfriend threw up in my car, I cleaned it to a tee. Not to mention the night I skied up on the police, I didn't have any drugs on me anyway, just the pistol.

The Police department was obviously upset at the fact that I'd gotten away and that there was nothing in the car they could charge me with. Surprisingly, I wasn't charged with evading arrest. They knew they were racially profiling me and didn't even have probable cause to pull e over.

I was relieved that this was the way they chosen to charge people. Send them a letter and allow them a chance to rectify minor infractions such as the ones that were written against me. It wasn't always necessary to take people away in handcuffs for misdemeanor code violations. These code violation list for moving violations and other petty crimes, such as being caught with less than an ounce of weed or drug paraphernalia. In these instances, the suspect would only be written a traffic ticket.

The one thing about these tickets is that they would have to be paid by the due date or be issued a warrant. These tickets prevented the jail from being crowded with petty criminals. They needed the jails to house the people who robbed, raped, stole and killed!

I always felt that the private and public companies that run the prisons also fund the police because the jails funnel criminals to them. So, in the past they took people who violated the codes to jail. It was like any other system. Even the school system. If there were no students, they'd have to shut them down. Not to mention the students who are singled out because they have no financial support. If the system considered them to be "economically" disadvantaged, then they were considered to "educationally" disadvantaged. These protocols determined how many future prisons should be built thinking the disadvantaged children would grow up to be criminals.

With the prisons that are built they fill them with people who commit petty crimes until they house the past potential criminals. This is a vicious cycle and

To avoid interruption in this systematic protocol, they allow the police to fill the jails with people who may have done nothing wrong. True wrong, Malum. (Malum in se a Latin term for naturally evil, such as

FREEDOM(E)

rob, rape or steal). They fill the jails with people that have done things (Malum prohibitum a Latin term which means wrong because prohibited).

Who has the authority to prohibit anyone born under God, the Sun, Moon and Stars! Have we appointed any to be the authority of us? The police are servants of the public which means we the people, are the public.

We are the ones who live our lives looking to enjoy liberty and freedom in the pursuit of happiness. If the truth be told, we are the authority over the police! Their job is to protect and serve us. We the people.

Knowing your rights is important. The police or any other law enforcement agent or any citizen may not put their hands on another unless they have witnessed that person commit a felony unless they are authorized by you to search them or their vehicle.

Even in the cases where a parent or guardian disciplines their child, God authorized them to bring the child into the world with the expectation that you would raise them right and teach them the difference between right and wrong. The first thing we teach them is to obey their parent or guardian so that they understand authority.

Considering all that had taken place, I decided not to rush to the court house. Later that week when I had some free time, I had my father take me to the police station to answer to the charges. I walked into the police station not knowing what to expect.

One thing for sure, I had never spent any time in jail besides the time I spent two weeks to lay out several traffic tickets. I was 17 years old, so it was a vague memory, but I remember not paying the ticket when it was initially due and was arrested and sent to jail. They'd called ahead asking for me not disclosing who they were. When I got to the phone, it was the police regarding the unpaid parking tickets. I should have listened to my gut when I realized the trickery involved in getting me on the phone. I agreed to come down and make payment arrangements.

When I walked in the police station, I headed for the clerk and told her I had just received a call to pay my unpaid parking tickets. She told me to have a seat and proceeded to make a phone call. The officer came up to me and instructed me to follow him down the corridor. When I got to the booking area, he told me to sit on the bench. The bench was old with paint that was chipped and peeling. I was truly wanting to take care of the tickets, I had no idea he would tell me to stand up, handcuff me and book me into the city jail.

Having been presented with the same opportunity to take care of charges by freely walking into the station made me apprehensive. I walked in the court house with the letter stating the misdemeanor charges against me.

I took a deep breath and walked up to the glass that the clerk sat behind. She asked if she could help me, and I tell her about the letter I'd gotten in the mail charging me with misdemeanor drug paraphernalia and no seat belt charges. I handed her the letter. She looked at the papers, then typed something on her keyboard. She then asks me how I wanted to plead.

FREEDOM(E)

I quickly answer, "Not guilty" knowing that I was not. She typed on her keyboard again then printed out a sheet of paper with my plea, the charges and a court date. Handing the paperwork to me she looked at me seriously and warned me to be there on the date stated.

I walked out in disbelief at not having been arrested, thinking to myself once again that this is how it should be done. Being walked into jails possibly with cameras should be reserved for serious crimes. Let alone this would decrease the rate that black men and people from urban communities being unnecessarily shot and killed by police.

When I walked back to the car where my father sat waiting, I broke into a big smile. It felt good to be walking out of the jail with nothing but a court date. Now this was due process! I felt good the rest of the day.

A few days later my father and I decided to go to the towing company that held my car. The towing company had also sent me a letter regarding the delinquency of my vehicle being claimed. They stated that the fees were fast accumulating. I didn't have the money to get my car off the towing company's lot, but I wanted my personal belonging out of the car.

As luck would have it, as I was freely walking (since I'd been cleared at the court house) to my parents to get a ride to the tow yard, when LDogg pulled up alongside me. I couldn't put my finger on it, but I didn't trust him at all. Since I was still at least a mile away from the house, I was reluctant to accept the ride because even though at this point I felt I couldn't be snitched on, there was still a slight hesitation getting into the vehicle.

He asked where I was headed, and I explained that although I could not afford to get my car out of the impound, I still needed to get my personal items from the vehicle. He offered to take me, and since I knew I'd need help transporting the items, I jumped in.

When we pulled into the parking lot, I jumped out the vehicle telling him I'd be right back. I walked into the office of the tow company and was met by a Korean man behind the counter. I told him my name and that I only needed to get my personal items out the car until I could afford to retrieve the vehicle.

He asked if I owned the Caprice. I nodded yes. I will never forget the look he had in his eyes as he led me out to the yard where all the vehicles were stored. I couldn't help but to think the smile and the look in his eyes indicated that he knew more about my vehicle and the circumstances than I could imagine.

When I unlocked the car door, I take a deep breath. I'm still pissed at the fact that this happened to me and now my very first vehicle was inaccessible. I looked the interior of my car over and saw a few things I wanted to grab. I opened the glove box and press the trunk release button. When the trunk popped open, I grabbed a few more things from there as well as an old milk crate I had in the back. I placed all the items I'd gathered from my car, handed the Korean clerk the keys, and proceeded to head back to LDogg's ride.

As soon as I turned the corner I see four or five police officers run from each end of the parking lot. I'm

FREEDOM(E)

shocked as they headed towards me. I patted my shirt pocket to make sure I still had my court papers on me. I didn't think they would be coming for me since I'd been released on the misdemeanor charges with a court date.

As I patted my left pocket on my shirt, all the policemen reached for their weapons. I realized I had on a different shirt without a pocket. With no pocket to reach into, I raised the one arm while my left hand held on the crate with my things.

The police, not knowing what was exactly in the crate, rushed me and instructed me to drop the crate and place both my hands in the air. They roughly placed my hands behind my back handcuffing me, then asking my name. I didn't answer. I was still in disbelief.

The police approached me and stated my name taking the crate form me placing it on the ground.

I looked at him in disbelief and said, "I went to the court building already, what is this about?"

The police man said to me "Remember when you ran?"

I said nothing. I knew it was best to keep my mouth shut as the officers surrounded me. I knew that Black men lost their lives in these situations, so I kept my cool.

I was taken to the city police station where I sat on the bench while they booked me in. They allowed me a phone call, so I phoned my parents telling them what had happened. They couldn't understand also. Although my parents couldn't understand, it was becoming clear to me. They had deceived me and tricked me by separating the "city" and "state" charges, hoping to bring me out from under. It worked. I thought I was home free after leaving the courthouse.

The next morning, they opened the cell door and escorted me back to the Judge's bench so that I could plead on the charge of evading arrest in a motor vehicle. Of course, I pled not guilty. They placed me back into the cell until the chain came to take all the inmates going from the city jail to the county jail. This time my wrists were cuffed to a belt around my waist and my feet cuffed as well! Damn "they" were steady pulling tricks out their sleeves.

We arrived at the county jail shortly after. I had been to this place a few times before, but that was a few times too many! We were all shoved into the same dirty, stinking holding cell I had been in when I came to jail my first time being locked down. This county jail looked as if it had the same blankets from six years ago and beyond. The blankets were musty and looked as if they were shot with buckshot rounds.

I choked down my anger and got situated making my bunk and storing my hygiene. Afterward, I lay on my bunk and just thought about the last time I felt true freedom while I slept. I knew that most of my problems were because I was always supporting and cheering on everyone else while I sat on the bench in my own life. It was time to at least get off the bench and into the stands. I had less than a handful of people outside of family that I could count on, but those who needed me could count on me. The force had always been with me. I learned a long time how to get along without. Get

FREEDOM(E)

along without people cheering for me or showing up to support things that mean the most to me.

That night I had a dream that I was in my old bedroom asleep. The dreams were lovely and comforting and I woke up feeling rested. I got off the bunk to stretch my legs and then walked over to the big glass window where all the jail announcements were posted.

I saw a poster that talked about a special type of PR Bond. If you didn't have any domestic violence crimes or 3 felony convictions, you could write to the address listed and apply for a PR Bond.

I knew I qualified for the PR Bond, so I asked the guard to bring me writing material so that I could apply. When I finished, I dropped the application in the outbox and went into the dayroom. I sat there patiently waiting on chow, but I was hoping and praying that I was getting out of here soon.

Being in jail this time is nothing like the other times I'd been locked down. Everybody sat around and told war stories attempting to gain glory, I wasn't feeling that. I stayed to myself and spoke only when spoken to. There was nothing glorious about being in this stink hole around people who were also lying and exaggerating.

So, I spent the next few days reading, writing, and sleeping a lot. The tanks in the county jail were terrible. They were very small, and the inmates only got recreation once a week. Being stuck in a small space with no fresh air was torture.

After a week my name was called. I stood at the call box praying they were about to tell me I was getting released. Five minutes later a guard walked me down the hall where a fat, white dude sat behind a desk. He asked me a few questions, but the only question I could remember is when he asked how I would feel about getting out today?

I told him I would be thankful. The man told me that I could get out that day if I signed the PR Bond. This meant I would have to be accountable to come back to court and answer for the evading arrest charge or a warrant would be issued. I was glad I had thought to apply.

I went back into the tank in a hurry to get roll my bunk and get my things together. Everybody was surprised when they saw me throwing away the county toothpaste and comb that I would no longer be needing. They wanted to know how I was getting out. I explained to them that I applied for a PR Bond and pointed to where the information was posted. A bunch of them went over to read the paper. I couldn't believe none of them had ever seen or read it.

An hour later I was released. It felt good to be breathing fresh air again even though I knew this ordeal wasn't over. I stopped by a store and bought some smokes and headed to a pay phone to call for a ride. I called my parents for a ride. My mother's sweet voice answered and was surprised when I told her I was released. She told me they were just about to come to the jail for a visit.

I found a spot to sit and wait and enjoyed looking at the cars going by and the cool breeze. Thirty minutes later I see my parent's car pull around the corner. I broke into

FREEDOM(E)

a huge smile and walked towards the car. They didn't see me at first and drove past me. I flagged them down and they pulled over so that I could jump in as I sit in the backseat behind my father, he nodded his head in approval saying "Hey, you're out!"

My mother looked back at me and smiled saying, "Hello my son!"

I greeted both my parents warmly and we drove to the house making small talk. My mother asked me more about how I was able to get released. I told her about the PR bond that I had to apply for. When she heard that I met the requirements she was happy to hear that.

CHAPTER FIVE

TRUTH SOMETIMES HURT

While in jail I had been doing some serious thinking; some reflecting. I thought long and hard about why I did the things that would get me into trouble. I knew I had become more depressed ever since moving to Texas. Living in a home without my father was the hardest. Having to move from the big city to the boon docks of Texas was hard also. This town was so slow. My new high school was extremely small, and most of the classrooms didn't have any windows. Coming from a big city, the windowless classrooms was unusual to me and I felt trapped.

I realized our family moving and my father staying behind to provide was very hard for me to cope with. On top of that, I had never seen the military up close before, only what I'd seen on movies and that was mostly gun fire and soldiers running. It became even harder when my father who was still in Massachusetts while we were in Texas was deployed to Iraq. Before he deployed I couldn't say good bye or tell him to be safe and come back to us.

During the ride home from the county jail I told my parents these things and how this affected a lot of my decisions. I told my father because I was so scared of losing him, I psychologically killed him in my own head by not thinking about him at all. I barely spoke to

FREEDOM(E)

him when we first moved to Texas and he stayed back in Massachusetts, and after he was deployed not at all.

So, I was 25 years old at the time, getting myself into unnecessary trouble when I had plenty of opportunities to make something of myself. Being in jail this time I felt I had finally found out why I had been acting out and I felt my parents deserved to know.

The rest of the twenty-five-minute ride home was silent. We drove the long country road back to the city. This was a winding road that only had one official stop sign. My parents had taken me home with them and I felt every negative vibe leaving my body as I stepped inside their home.

I had no worries. Nothing could get to me. I took my shoes off in the vestibule per my mother's wishes then headed to the guest room, peeled off my clothes, and jumped in the shower. I could feel and smell how dirty I was. As I scrubbed the county jail off me, I once again thought how thankful I was to have my loving parents. They have made a firm foundation for me and my siblings to stand and I'm sure that couldn't be easy, especially with my nonsense behavior. I realized that many of my peers live and had grown some for the better and some the worse, but most were raised in single parent households. Some of those friends of mine were single parents themselves. The warm water ran down my body and the sudsy water bounced off my body hitting the shower walls. From my head to the tips of my toes, I could feel each drop forming flowing cleansing streams making their way down my body.

JASON MCMILLAN

I stepped out of the shower and put on one of my father's tee shirts and pants that I borrowed. I didn't keep clothes at my parents' house, so I had no other choice and I didn't mind. My parents were in the family room watching television. I walked through the family room into the kitchen and opened the refrigerator looking for something to eat. I grabbed a bagel and made a sandwich.

After eating, I joined my parents in the family room, spending quality time with them so they wouldn't think I was taking them for granted. After the hard stools in the county jail, the softness of my mother's couch seemed to be the softest couch in the world. We sat around watching movies until I passed out on the couch. The next morning, I woke up to the smell of breakfast cooking. My mother had made breakfast for us all and afterwards, my parents drove me to the apartment I shared with my sister which wasn't too far from my parents' home. When we arrived, I thanked them and headed into my apartment.

When I stepped into the apartment, it felt as if I hadn't been there in forever. It was like going back to visit the old high school you graduated from and when you looked around everything that once seemed so big was a lot smaller. I got dressed into my own clothes and headed out the back door to the corner store. The corner store was the only place I knew of that had a working pay phone. I dialed my brothers cell phone and he finally answered on the fourth ring. When he answered, I grinned and asked him what was good? I knew I'd caught him by surprise due to the fact he hadn't heard from me in over a month.

FREEDOM(E)

He was happy and asked how I'd gotten out so quickly.
I went through the spill about getting the PR bond and
he was hyped about coming to see me.

"Where you at?" He asked impatiently.

I told him I was at my apartment and he told me he
would be pulling up. I was enthused by his excitement.
We both knew it was about to be on!

Before long, I heard Prince's car pulling up. I rushed to
unlock the door and greeted my brother with a bear hug
and a dap. As soon as we made our way inside he
pulled out a pre-rolled blunt and lit up. We smoked and
laughed while I told him about my recent escapade in
jail. A thought had sparked. I asked my brother if he
knew anyone that would buy the gun I had stashed or
trade me for a decent amount of bud for it. If I was
going to make a deal like this, I would only do it
through my brother because I knew I could trust him.

My brother also knew I could trust him and that I had
his back too. A few months before the entire incident
involving me and the state troopers, my brother was
robbed at gun point while dealing drugs. He called to
ask me for a "burner" but sadly I didn't have a gun on
me then. I told him that I'd make a few phone calls and
call him back.

While I was searching through my contacts I thought
about all the attempts that have been made on my life. I
should have taken them all as wake-up calls and should
have made better decisions, but I couldn't see the
wrong in my actions. I thought I was being as cool as
everyone else in my crowd.

JASON MCMILLAN

One of the things I will always regret is that one of my younger brothers followed my street lifestyle. I should have been setting an example, but I was setting the wrong kind. He was always wanting to tag along. One night we hooked up with a couple of chicks from the neighborhood. They drove up and we jumped in tying bandanas over our face. These chicks were my homegirls. They were down with us. No matter what we needed to do, we knew that we could count on them. I had also set a bad example for young women.

They let us out after we discussed the spot they would come back and pick us up. We went to hit up some other dudes that were trying to run our block. As soon as we got to their territory, I let loose with my semi-automatic handgun. My brother had a smaller caliber gun but was just as eager to shoot. I hate the day we did that. Less than a month later, my youngest brother was killed by a bullet shot through his bedroom window.

These thoughts intermingled with my brother Prince being robbed had me seriously thinking about how the street life was taking us black men out, one by one.

My brother shook my arm, bringing me out of my deep thoughts telling me that one of his homeboys was willing to trade me an ounce of weed for the gun.

I placed the pistol into a backpack and we jumped into the car heading up the street to his homeboy's house. We get out of the car and head inside. I dap the homie then reach into the backpack placing the pistol on the counter top. At the same time, homeboy is weighing the ounce of weed. I was happy that I was getting some weed, and I'm also happy that my brother watched me

FREEDOM(E)

make a better decision to get rid of the gun, then to get in anymore trouble keeping it.

After the weed was weighed out, I stuffed the ounce into my pocket and me and my brother dipped. We arrived at my apartment a few minutes later. As soon as we got inside, I pulled out the trees and roll a blunt. As we inhaled and exhaled the smoke, I rested my head back on the recliner and tried to concentrate on just relaxing. My brother got up to leave after we'd smoked a couple of blunts. I wanted to chill some more. I didn't want to think any negative thoughts or think about my impending court case. I knew I still had to check with my bondsman to find out my court date. I made a mental note of it as I inhaled and exhaled more smoke.

CHAPTER SIX

GET OUT AND GET SOMETHING

The following next weeks were spent with me spending my days at the local library, filling out job applications and searching the internet. After leaving the library, I would walk into a lot of the local establishments looking for work. I kept getting hit with the same answer from each of the employers, "We are reviewing your application and will get back to you."

No calls had come.

I was trying not to get frustrated. I knew it wasn't going to be easy, but I was determined to bounce back. I knew I had to keep looking.

It had been two months that I hadn't been able to contribute my portion to the bills and I'm sure my sister counted on my income.

One day, I while riding with my mother, she told me about a family she knew that had opened a restaurant and was looking for workers. My mother told me that she met the owners at an event and that I should go down and talk to the owners myself.

A few days later, I'd gotten dressed up in slacks and a nice dress shirt and went to the family-owned restaurant. I brought an extra shirt in case I needed to change. The restaurant was at least a 30-minute walk.

FREEDOM(E)

When I arrived, I noticed that the establishment was busy, and the workers were hustling about trying to appease the large crowd.

I looked around for a manager but noticed two men heading out the service entrance getting into a vehicle. I recognized one of the young men. He was someone I went to school with. He nodded his head acknowledging he knew who I was as I approached their car. I told him that I was there to apply for a job. He told me to come back tomorrow and he was sure they would hire me.

I went home that evening and called a homeboy to solidify a ride for the next day and fell fast asleep. I woke up the next morning and ate a quick breakfast, showered, and was waiting at the door when my homie drove up.

He had a few other homeboys with him and said he hoped that I didn't mind. I was cool with it, I just needed a ride. We headed to the restaurant and before I hopped out of the car one of his homeboys asked if I could buy him something to eat inside. I wouldn't have minded if I was getting myself something and had the cash, I'd get us all something. But this wasn't the case, so I looked at him crazy and told him I came here to make money, not spend money!

When I stepped inside, I go up to the employee behind the counter and asked for a job application. She handed me the application, I thanked her, then sat down at a nearby table to fill it out. It didn't take long. The application was only a front/back sheet of paper.

JASON MCMILLAN

After I finished the application I handed it to the employee and asked if I could speak with the manager. Moments later an older woman comes to the counter. I introduced myself to her extending my hand to shake hers. I told her that I didn't want to take up too much time, but that I was looking for a job and would like the opportunity to work there.

She told me she'd review my application and give me a call. A few days later I was called in for an official interview then hired on the spot.

The job was nice, the employer was great, but my fellow team members were awesome. We all worked together and never seemed to have any problems with each other. I worked hard for them for four months. One day, I overslept by 20 minutes. I rushed to my neighbor's apartment knocking on their door asking to use their telephone.

I called the job and the phone just rang and rang. My calls went unanswered.

I rushed and got dressed as quickly as I could. I shot out of the apartment, rushing down the steps, and jogging up the street to work. When I arrived, the manager looked at me and said, "You're late and you should have called."

I explained to her that I did call, but the phone just rang and rang. She glared at me and accused me of lying. I was heated. The first thing I did was tried to call to tell them I would be late. I wanted to walk off, but I knew that I needed the job. I was even more pissed when she told me to just go home and check the schedule next week. I left there and never came back until it was time

FREEDOM(E)

for me to pick up my last paycheck. After being call a lair and being treated that way, I couldn't care less about my employment with them. I didn't want to work with them anymore!

I started looking for things to do, staying busy. I cleaned my apartment from top to bottom and organized all my belongings. After a few days of this, I decided to go by and visit my mother. I called her beforehand to ask if I could stop by.

"Absolutely my son!" She said sweetly.

When I arrived, she greeted me at the door with a big hug and a kiss. She asked if I wanted anything to eat. She knew I did. She fixed me a plate and I followed her into the family where we sat and made small talk while I ate. There was nothing like mama's cooking. Just as I had gotten ready to savor another bite, I noticed a car creeping down the block through my mother's blinds.

CHAPTER SEVEN
CRY FOR HELP

I walked into the dining room to get a closer look. I recognized the dark SUV. It was Kamara. I had met her a few months before the police chase. She came around from the driver's side with a hopeful look on her face as she walked up to the front door to knock.

I opened the door before she could, greeting her with a friendly smile.

"What's up girl?" I asked, genuinely happy to see her.

She told me that she had been going through a lot and really needed a friend. She told me that one night she'd been drinking and had gotten so drunk that she passed out leaving her one-year old son unattended. He had gotten out of the house while she was passed out and had been found across five lanes of traffic at the local corner store. Authorities were called and until their investigation was complete she needed someone to be with her under 24-hour supervision. Since I was seeking employment, I figured we could help each other.

At the time I didn't know that she had only told me half the story involving the incident with her son. She now lived in the next city over and I figured I may have a better chance finding employment in the city she lived. Plus, she had always been a good friend and I loved her and her two children. I remember once she had a surgery and I would go to her apartment to check on her

FREEDOM(E)

after her procedure. I was looking forward to getting out of the city and searching this new city for work. I also looked forward to having my friend by my side and us helping each other in the process. I knew she never had any ill intentions, so I figured it was all good.

I jumped in the SUV after going to my apartment packing clothes and hygiene and everything else I was taking with me and took off on the highway. I was ready to get "on my feet" so I didn't waste any time.

I was happy and excited looking forward to this new opportunity and moving forward. I was also looking forward to supporting my friend. We were going to support each other. It was the twenty-four-hour supervision requirement fulfillment that allowed her to keep custody of her two children. So, I was happy I could help my friend, a beautiful Black Queen, keep custody of her offspring. She also seemed just as happy to be able to help me with my job search.

When we arrived at her home she took her children inside and I began bringing in my things. Shortly after settling in she made herself a drink. She continued to pour drink after drink, downing one after the other. I didn't think anything of it because I was feeling such a euphoria at the thought of us partnering up and coming through for each other.

The next day I rode with her while she took care of some things with her children. We went to the clinic which took most of the day, so I planned to go job hunting the next day. That evening, I sat down at the kitchen table and took out my notebook. I began journaling my experiences and feelings. Once she got the children settled, she lit a cigarette and asked if I'd like a drink. I figured it couldn't have been easy being a single parent with two children, one of which, the daughter, had special needs. I accepted her offer and thought about my plan of action for job search the next day.

When she initially approached me with the opportunity she'd only told me her son had gotten out of the house while she was sleeping. It was obvious to me that she had a drinking problem and was probably blacked out when the incident happened. I wanted to help her, but I sure didn't want to enable her.

That evening before bed, she and I planned our following day. She had a few things lined up and I had mentioned stopping by a food market I'd seen earlier that day. The next morning, we got dressed and headed out to run her errands. Before heading back to the house, we pulled into the food market. I immediately got out of the vehicle and into the building to the customer service counter.

I asked the employee behind the counter if I could speak with a manager. A few minutes later the manager appeared. I greeted him with my biggest smile and let him know that I was looking for a job. I let him know that I was currently trying to get back on my feet and that I would be willing to work any shift in any role.

He appeared to have an interest by responding positively to everything I told him. He handed me an application and told me that he couldn't make any promises but that he would be willing to look it over.

I was ecstatic. All I needed was one shot.

FREEDOM(E)

I walked back to Kamara's SUV with my head held even higher than before. I had a great feeling about this place and it was just down the street from her home so that was a bonus. I know she wouldn't mind helping me though I knew the less I needed from her the better I could do for myself. Anything could come up when you have two small children. So, I could see that having a job close to her place coming in handy in many ways.

When we arrived at her home, I sat down and immediately filled out the application while Kamara fixed the children's dinner. After preparing the meal, she fixed herself a drink. I was beginning to pick up on her pattern.

One day her social workers stopped by for a house visit to set up special services for her disabled child. Knowing how important this was, I went into Kamara's bedroom and gently shook her awake, letting her know that social workers were in the front room. When she finally realized what I was saying, her dazed eyes widened frantically. She was severely hung over but tried to gather her senses as she walked into the family room where the social workers were already interviewing her daughter.

Kamara attempted to put on her best smile while interacting with the social workers. She answered all their questions and gave specific information on her daughter Ashley's behavior. Although I wasn't listening closely, I was paying attention to the demeanor and glances the social workers had amongst each other.

The meeting lasted about a half an hour and the two women social workers left. Despite her disheveled appearance and slightly slurred speech, the social workers agreed to get Ashley the help she needed to get into the special school.

We did our best with the children. I could always make Ashley smile by taking her outside and grabbing her arms swinging and spinning her in circles. She loved that and nee. After spinning her she would get dizzy then walk as fast as she could back to me grabbing my hands signaling for me to spin her again and again. She couldn't pronounce words, but he sure could laugh and smile though, and I was great at making her do that. Kamara's son also loved to play with me. He would bring his toys to me and convince me to play with him. I didn't mind. I loved that brought his favorite things to me. His basketball and his favorite toy car.

The days were long and endless. Every so often, I would go in and ask to speak to the hiring manager at the food market. Each time I went in, I was told that the hiring manager wasn't available. I never stopped trying. One day, the hiring manager happened to be at the counter. He'd obviously been told how often I stopped by and agreed to offer me an interview. I was so grateful, happy, and ready.

Thing's at Kamara's were starting to become more challenging. Kamara had deeper issues than just the drinking. There was something causing her to drink as she did, but she wouldn't open herself up to share with me about it. I didn't know how to help her.

FREEDOM(E)

The television was always on and seemed to be taking the place of raising the children. They stared at the TV for hours. I wish I could look at it so hard that it would explode into a million pieces never to be watched again.

A few days before my interview the special needs therapist made a visit. Ashley was sitting on the couch rocking as she did most of the time. Kamara immediately opened the door for the therapist. I was glad she wasn't passed out or hungover this time.

When the therapist walked in I couldn't help but notice she was a beautiful, plus-size black woman who carried herself well, what we call "thick" in the hood.

We made introductions and she walked over to where Ashley sat. The therapist reached out to shake Ashley's hand to see what type of response she'd get. Ashley looked at her with a blank stare and continued rocking.

The teacher reached into her bag and brought out a tube with various shaped holes as well as the plastic shapes designed to fit each hole. She brought the cube to Ashley and began to fill in some of the matching pieces. She would take each piece and hand them to Ashley with hopes that she'd do the same. Although Ashley smiled, she wouldn't participate. She would let the piece fall out of her hand and then burst into hysterical laughter. The therapist tried to engage her with more activities then handed a sheet of paper to Kamara with a list of exercises to go over at home.

The therapist scheduled for the next week and as soon as she walked out the door, Kamara poured a huge drink. It was becoming more and more difficult for Kamara to control her drinking. It was obviously affecting her ability to parent her children and give Ashley the much-needed attention she deserved.

One evening I was sitting at the dining table writing, Kamara was in the kitchen cooking, and Ashley was sitting on the couch rocking back and forth. Remembering the box of shapes the therapist left, I got up and got them and sat on the couch to play with her. This was the first time I'd seen her play with toys. In fact, the day the therapist came by was the first day anyone had ever interacted with her in such a way. She played and kept smiling at me. Her smile was beautiful. I spent quite a bit time playing with her hoping the next time the therapist came she would see a difference. For some reason, I felt I had a special connection with this child. It made me feel good inside that I was helping to teach her, and the double blessing would be teaching her mother to teach her.

Something would have to give soon. The longer I stayed at Kamara's the more I felt that my priorities were getting pushed to the side. I never got to really follow up with the food market and by the time I got to, they'd hired someone else. I wasn't discouraged about not getting the job, but I was becoming increasingly frustrated with Kamara and her drinking habit. She would pass out every night and/or be hungover the next morning, so I ended up being the babysitter, the maid, etc. and I was still no closer to reaching my own goals.

She cried out for help, but she didn't want someone to help her, she wanted someone to enable her.

FREEDOM(E)

CHAPTER EIGHT

BRO COME GET ME! 911!

One-night Kamara got unusually drunk. She was on the phone with her sister. When I realized it was her sister on the phone, I threw out an off-handed compliment which Kamara took the wrong way. Even after the phone call, Kamara kept raging about what I'd said. I kept trying to explain to her that she was taking everything the wrong way, but she'd been drinking so much that evening, that she was damn near incoherent.

An hour later, still drunk, Kamara was still ranting about what I'd said. She was working herself up into a frenzy and I tried to calm her down several times. Finally, she screamed at me that I was like her babies' daddies. I screamed back at her that I wasn't their daddy but that I was apparently doing a better job than they were. She didn't handle this statement too well and escalated to coming close and yelling in my face. She was clapping her hands and screaming and all I could think is if this was going to get any crazier. Kamara was most-definitely out of control. What if she picked up a knife? I didn't know what she'd do.

I decided it was best for me to leave. I had begun to be concerned with my safety. I called my brother and asked him if he could come and get me 911! He knew that meant come RIGHT NOW. He told me to give him a few minutes and he would be on his way. I thanked him and hung up. I immediately began to pack my things. All I could grab at the time were a few changes of clothing, but I would come back for the rest later. I had the feeling that the sooner I left the better.

After I had the things I would take with me, I sat on the porch to wait outside for my brother. Forty-five minutes later he showed up. I got in the car and he took me home. Damn it sucked I had to leave her like that. I couldn't stay in her place with her feeling like my life could be in jeopardy. I hoped she got to the root of her troubles and wake up. I had problems too! Hell, I wasn't even close to perfect. Which is why I always try my best to reflect on life and make immediate changes.

Things in my life had now gone back to square one. I was back in town. I had court coming up for the two trumped-up charges from the city for driving with no set belt and drug paraphernalia and still had to face court on the impending evading arrest charges. I had no job and no income.

When I went to court they told me that if I plead guilty to the drug paraphernalia charge they would dismiss the driving with no seat belt charge and I'd only be fined. Damn that was fucked up, especially knowing neither of these charges are true. The police are some real bullies don't let anyone fool you! Even knowing the truth, I sat and considered this devil lady's offer.

I explained to her that I hadn't had success finding a job and I didn't want to agree to a payment arrangement that I couldn't afford. The judge asked me had I heard of Labor Ready which is day labor for people in need of work. The day labor center was in the city I'd just left with Kamara. I didn't know how I would get back and forth daily.

FREEDOM(E)

Just wanting to get out of these people faces, I agreed and after I don't think I could have gotten out of that place any faster. I was glad things were beginning to settle. Even though I know the system was bullying me, what was a man to do?

Visiting with my mother always helps, so I walked over to my parent's home. As soon as I walked in the door, every negative feeling I had seemed to evaporate into thin air. My mother's home was a safe place. Her words were therapeutic, and she always gave such wise advice. She and I brainstormed ideas on how I could to and from the day labor center. I was so ready to be done with all this mess that I was willing to ride a bike up the highway. My mother discouraged me from that thought saying it wouldn't be safe, but she thought to call a friend of the family who was a real estate agency and ask for a favor. She asked if there was an apartment I could rent with the little amount of money I had. It wasn't much but she shared my plans on how I was going to get on my feet by being so close to the day labor center and would pay any back-owed rent.

We decided to go and check out the day labor center before I signed a lease on an apartment. When we arrived in front of the day labor building, there were a few young brothers out front shooting dice. I'd seen this all before so seeing brothers shooting dice was nothing new. I did know that dice games can also lead to trouble, especially when you're winning, and my dice game was strong. I was here to earn legit cash, so I walked around the brothers without looking back, determined not to allow myself to become distracted.

I wondered what my mother was thinking as we walked past the dice game and into the center. I spoke to the clerk at the counter asking her how to apply. She explained the process and told me that I needed to come back the next day and bring 2 form of ID, but that I could go ahead and take the hiring test now since I was already there. I took the test and passed.

A couple of days later my mother took me to the day labor center with the required identification to complete the application process. I was now registered with the center and ready to earn some cash. I knew it wouldn't be easy. I spent all the money I had moving to the new apartment. I had no money left to even turn on the utilities. I wanted to pay off my debt and the realtor who helped me get the apartment. I knew my money would be tight for a while.

I returned to my old apartment to pack some things. I packed all my clothes and hygiene and a couple of gallons of water. I called my brother and asked if he could help me move my things. He told me that he could and would be over shortly. My brother was always there for me. I didn't know how I'd ever repay him.

When my brother dropped me off at my new apartment, I immediately went in and put away the few items I had. After saying goodbye to my bro, I set my battery-operated alarm clock and slept on the bare floor. I didn't have a blanket or pillow. It sucked because I felt like I was back in jail fighting for freedom. Freedom(e).

The next morning, I woke up at five a.m. to make sure I'd be one of the first workers in the line. They

FREEDOM(E)

recruited workers for the jobs on a first come/first serve basis. Nothing was guaranteed.

When I arrived, there were already 10 people in line. "Damn!" I thought to myself. They must have gotten up at 4 a.m. At 6am the doors to the facility opened and we filed in one by one, stopping to sign the sign in sheet and be issued a number.

I vowed to remain optimistic and waited patiently in my seat. The hours slowly ticked by and they'd only called 4 or 5 workers out. It was one o'clock and I figured they wouldn't get anymore dispatches for work today. I still left with a positive mindset. I was going to come back the next day even earlier so that I'd be one of the first in line.

When I arrived at my new apartment, I sat outside in the sun enjoying the weather, and watched the sunset. I went in, washed up, and laid down. I wanted to go to sleep early so that I could wake up refreshed and ready.

I awoke to the sound of my alarm clock buzzing. I shivered after having to sleep in my pants and undershirt using my sweatshirt as a pillow. I got up and grabbed a towel and one of the gallons of water and quickly washed my face, brushed my teeth, and headed out the door.

I showed up 45 minutes earlier than I had the day before. There were still 5 people already in line. We stood there waiting for the doors to open. Just as the day before, the doors opened promptly at 6 a.m. and we filed in to complete the sign in process. Some of the workers had priorities over others due to specialized skills and certain certifications. I sat straight up in my seat with my head held high, waiting and hoping to be called for work. Just as the day before, I waited till after 1 p.m. and still hadn't been called. Knowing there'd be no more dispatches for the day, I went home to repeat the same routine as I had the previous day. As I lay on the hard floor I thought about how much harder this was going to be than I'd initially thought.

Getting up earlier and earlier was becoming increasingly frustrating. I had no idea what time I needed to be there to be first in line. The next morning, routine repeated, I arrived to see people in line already. Once again, I'd wait till 1 p.m. to see if I'd be called. Stepping outside to have a smoke, I noticed a white Crown Victoria pull up in the parking lot. I'd seen it circle through the parking lot through the huge windows of the building.

I watched as the brother exited the vehicle and entered the building to the counter. He stepped away from the counter quickly like he was running late for something. As he walked past me, he quickly asked me did I want to work. I said yes just as quickly and followed him to his car.

We introduced ourselves as we sped down the highway. He told me his name was Tony and went on to explain that he worked for a privately-owned landscaping company. He was instructed by the owner to find a worker to help lay sod on the lawns of a new duplex development. I was glad to hear it and I told him.

I shared with him how I had been trying my best to get to the center early enough to get work and stuck around

FREEDOM(E)

till the afternoon but hadn't had any luck getting dispatched thus far.

He told me how he'd started at the labor center and my tenacity demonstrated I was motivated to find some work. Immediately I could tell that he saw something in me. When we pulled into the housing development, I noticed the lawns of the brand-new units covered in dirt. Tony asked if I'd ever laid said before. I told him that I had, and he assured me that if the owner liked my work, there was a possibility I could be hired directly through the company.

There were several pallets of sod in the driveway. He told me that there was a specific way he wanted it laid. After demonstrating the method in which he wanted it done, I surprisingly picked up on it quickly and we breezed through 3 yards.

We worked throughout the day and when we finished, we cleaned up and got into his vehicle. He asked where I needed to go, and I told him to just drop me back off at the center. When we arrived, he handed me sixty dollars and asked if I wanted to work again the next day. I assured him that I did and walked in the center smiling, happy to have been paid well for an honest day's work.

After checking a few things, I headed home to my apartment. I still had no electricity and had been eating crackers and peanut butter sandwiches to survive. This day I decided to splurge and went to a fast food place and treated myself to a warm meal. I had to remember to use the bathroom whenever I was out because I still had no water. The food was delicious and as I went home to prepare for my next day.

Things were looking up and I was determined to keep the momentum going. That night as I slept on my floor, I had a smile on my face. I knew the next day I had an opportunity to work again and didn't have to be concerned with the sign in and wait process at the day labor center.

When I arrived at the center, I stepped aside from the line of people forming at the door. Once again, I felt grateful for having met Tony. Fifteen minutes later I see the white Crown Victoria making its way through the parking lot. Gerald told me we were going to be laying sod as we did yesterday. I had no problem with it. I was ready to earn my keep.

We had pulled up to another new development. When we got there, he noticed the sod hadn't arrived. After making a call to the delivery driver, we sat down to smoke a couple of cigarettes until the truck pulled up.

When the truck arrived with two full pallets of sod, we didn't waste any time getting to work. We weren't on a time schedule, so the sooner we finished, the sooner we could go leave for the day. It wasn't hard. We were done by 2 p.m.

Gerald had told me on the way to drop me off that there would be work the next day. He told me that we'd be working on a different project. This day I had him drop me off my apartment. Before I got out of the car I told him that I was interested in working the new project. He told me not to worry about walking to the center; that he would pick me up from my apartment in the

FREEDOM(E)

morning. That was cool. I wouldn't have to get up as early in the morning and I wouldn't have to walk the mile and a half to the center. Plus, it was still a great felling knowing that I had something lined up and I wouldn't have to sit and wait. Not that I minded though like I said, nothing was guaranteed.

Just as I had the previous night, I went to have a warm meal for dinner at the local fast food joint, making sure to use the bathroom before I left. Going home with my stomach full and positive thoughts going on in my heart and mind, I forgot all my troubles, just for that moment. When I arrived at my apartment, I sat on the steps just out front of the building and savored the sun until it set.

I woke up as soon as my alarm went off. I had a little pep in my stop because it was Friday and I was ready to end my week on a good note and enjoy my weekend. When Gerald's car pulled up, I bounded down the stairs and got into his car. After we greeted each other, Gerald explained that we would be digging trenches for sprinkler systems and would be digging huge holes where trees and bushes would eventually be planted. I didn't mind. I was ready to do whatever I needed to do to continue making money.

I didn't realize how hard the work was. This was *"real"* labor. After we dug holes for the trees and bushes, we installed the sprinkler systems. Gerald appreciated the fact that all he had to do was show me something once and I would catch on quickly. Today was going to be a full day's work and I wasn't complaining.

I stayed focused on the job and the time just seemed to fly by. After cleaning up and heading home, Gerald assured me he would be there to get me early Monday morning. I happily told him I'd be up and waiting!

After being home a few hours, my parents came to pick me up so that I could spend the weekend with them. I wasn't all the way in the door before I grabbed my back pack and headed straight to the bathroom to shower. Feeling better, I dropped all my dirty clothes in the washer and started the load of laundry. Things were getting better by the day and it felt good to have hot water streaming down my body; muscles sore from all the manual labor. My parents were in the kitchen cooking and soon the food was ready. We sat down and had dinner and talked and laughed at the table. It was great. Times were always great at my parents' house. What was even better is that I was able to tell them I had been working regularly. It made me happy to see the look of pride in their eyes.

After dinner we sat in the family room and watched movies for the rest of the evening. The next morning my mother was up at the crack of dawn. Saturday was the day she tended her garden. This Saturday was no different. I got up and quickly washed my face and brushed my teeth finishing just as she walked out the door. I caught the door before it closed and she looked back and saw me ready to come out and help. Once again, she smiled with pride, but the pleasure was all mine. I always enjoyed working on projects with my mother, especially with her lawn and garden. She and I would get on our hands and knees and pull weeds, toil soil, and plant flowers and other shrubbery.

The garden in the front of the house also needed tending. There was one type of flower that would shed

FREEDOM(E)

its petals daily and the petals would become seed for a new flower. We had to pick up the petals often to make sure the flowers don't grow out of control. I sat about the task of picking up the flower petals and raking up leaves.

By then the early morning sun was coming out. It would be getting hot soon, so mother and I decided to go in, have breakfast, and come back out in the cool of the evening and finish up.

After breakfast I heard my father and a friend preparing to work on a project on the house and I asked if they needed another hand. My father appreciated me volunteering to help them and we finished the job faster than they would have had I not. When the job was done, my father and I hung out for the rest of the day. When we got home, my mother was already outside in the garden. My father went inside while I stayed outside to give my mother a hand. It felt good to be able to help my parents around their house.

Sunday, we slept in and ate a huge brunch. I gathered my clean laundry and some other things I'd left at my parents' house the last time I was there. I also left with some supplies: 2 five-gallon paint buckets for packing water, a cooler, and a sleeping bag. I grabbed a blanket and pillow and was once again grateful that things were looking up.

My parents dropped me off later that evening. This is how my weekends went for a while. My father told me when he was free he would take me to get my bed and things from my old apartment. I had gotten out of the truck with my items and my father helped me with my things into the building. Then he told me he would see me later. It was night time, with no lights inside my apartment. I unrolled my sleeping bag and called it a night.

On Monday morning when I opened my eyes, I suddenly remembered how hard the floor was. My back and legs were hurting from the wooden floor in addition to my muscles being sore from the past work week. I was truly grateful, but life was still hard. I was still having to carry water to flush toilets and clean my body.

I was able to work with Gerald's landscaping crew for the rest of the week and I finally had enough money to get my electricity turned on. I was super happy to have lights and a refrigerator and a way to heat water on the stove instead of always having to wash up with the cold water from the buckets.

On Friday after finishing our work day. Gerald handed me my pay and I was excited to be able to see some more hard-earned cash. As I took off my safety vest and goggles and waited for my parents to arrive to come and get me for the weekend, I thought briefly about how Gerald didn't mention anything about Monday. Little did I know that that was the end of it. I got dropped off at my apartment building and hadn't seen Gerald since.

I heard my father's truck pull up and a knock on the door shortly thereafter. Opening the door and greeting my dad, I grabbed my laundry basket as my dad grabbed my backpack and we headed to the car. That weekend was like all the others. I helped my father with

FREEDOM(E)

projects around the house, my mother with her gardening, did laundry, ate, slept, and relaxed. That night after my dad brought me home, I walked to the corner store for smokes and a beer. I smoked a few cigs and drank my beer and before long I was out like a light.

Early the next morning I awoke to the buzzing of my alarm clock. Reminded by my aching bones of how hard the floor was, I stretched my sore body and yawned loudly. When my father dropped me off the night before, he allowed me to bring the small refrigerator as well. He brought all my clothing up while I brought in the refrigerator, plugged it up, and smiled. Things were looking up. My father said he would return the following week in his truck to get my bed, dresser, loveseat, and television from my old apartment to my new one.

After getting dressed I grabbed my bike and headed out for the day labor center. I wanted to make sure I was still registered. I was. The next morning and every morning thereafter, I arrived at the center and was beginning to get there and be one of the first five people to sign in.

I noticed the same brothers that were shooting dice were still there. They were still doing the same thing, walking around talking loud with their pants sagging. I was always going to be a black man, but I wanted to make sure I didn't fall into the category of being a "nigga"

I eventually found work through the day labor center. I was here to earn cash and let my name be known through my character and work ethic. While stacking my cash, I kept in touch with the court clerk to find out what day I would be in court regarding my evading arrest. The first offer she mentioned was four years of incarceration, which of course I turned down. The second time she came back with an offer of two years.

FREEDOM(E)

CHAPTER NINE

HOME SWEET HOME

I was still living at my new place without running water. I would fill my five-gallon paint buckets at my parent's house on the weekend. Eventually, my parents changed their schedule and couldn't pick me up in the city on Fridays anymore. I would always pay close attention to the weather and try not to forget to place my buckets outside for rain water. I hoped my neighbors didn't notice my pattern.

I practiced meditation to keep my emotional balance in check. I was working hard and earned money, but it was always spent before I earned it. With rent, electricity, and court fines, I had so many financial obligations that no matter how much I brought in, it was never enough. One of the jobs I landed through day labor paid such good money. It lasted over thirty days and I was paid $80 daily after taxes.

I lived like this for almost a year. I had another pretrial court date coming up and although I had a good run with the labor center for the summer, during the fall and winter jobs slowed down gradually. It was something we all knew and could tell was approaching. I had been putting money to the sided for the few months and put away whatever I would manage to save. I was determined to earn money in as many ways I could. I was cutting grass and was cleaning apartments, doing small renovations and plumbing jobs for my apartment complex in exchange for rent or cash.

The winter was cold. I would be wrapped up in my thermal blanket or would sit by the space heater. January couldn't come faster. Pretrial court happens the whole year and every time I'd go in for my court date they reset it. One morning after heating a pot of water for coffee and washing up, I got dressed for pretrial court.

I straightened my apartment while waiting for my father to pull up. After he arrived, I locked up and got into the car, surprised to see my mother in the car. She told me that she wouldn't miss an important court date and I was happy that she wanted to support me. We made the hour drive to the courthouse. We made small talk along the way. They were telling me how proud of me they were and how much they liked my apartment. I was proud. I knew my apartment wasn't much, but I'd come a long way and it would only get better.

When we arrived at the courthouse I went inside the foyer to meet with my attorney. My attorney advised me that the DA was offering me a one-year sentence. I rejected the idea immediately. There was no way I was signing for prison time. My attorney told me she would go in to talk to the District Attorney and judge to see if they'd give me a different offer. She returned saying the judge wouldn't move past a 6-month sentence.

As I pondered over whether to accept the offer I thought back to all the mistakes I'd made. All the previous bad choices I made were made on a whim. I thought I should have learned by now. I decided to go

FREEDOM(E)

ahead and sign for the time. I'd been free for a year and I had an opportunity to stack some cash and accomplish a few things, so I signed for the 6-month sentence.

Although it wasn't easy to make the decision, the charge of Attempted Evading Arrest with a Motor Vehicle was a serious one, so I figured with all things considered, this was the best decision. I had made the decisions to do wrong and now it was time to face the consequences. Noticeably, I should have never picked up the gun in the first place. I needed to repent. I vowed that I would start learning from my mistakes, so I had to trust my gut as they placed the handcuffs on me in front of my parents.

I didn't come to court today expecting to sign a deal. Because we were still in pretrial, I had expected to go home. I wanted to go home free, but I would not be going home that day. Damn it wasn't easy! I felt a little better because although my "time" was just being, I felt more freedom(e) than I had in all my life. I was tired of looking over my shoulders and trying hard to stay out of trouble so that I wouldn't add anymore charges to my already pending case.

This was the beginning of the end. I knew I had to be locked down and serve the time, but afterwards I'd be free to make better choices. I wouldn't have to look over my shoulder anymore. I was about to experience freedom(e) on a different level.

CHAPTER TEN

FREEDOM(E) TO CHANGE

Committing to one's self to change is the biggest first step in acquiring one's goals. That's what I had to tell myself as I signed the deal for the time. I told myself that this would not last forever and when I get out, nothing will stop me from becoming the greatest that I could be. I will be my own boss by doing what I love to do and getting paid to do it. I wanted to work and travel the world simply by the fruits of my labor.

A lot of those thoughts were running through my head. I look over to my left where my mother was standing looking upset at the sight of me in handcuffs. I spoke quietly to her "Six months. Not that long. Come visit me once a month and the time will go by faster!" Hoping to get rid of some of the negativity of the moment. To show her I still would hold my head up as best I knew how. And learn new ways.

She told me they would come visit more than once a month and walked away sadly as the officers said they were getting ready to take me away. I got a hug from my mother before they escorted me from the courthouse to the van waiting to transport me to the jail.

I looked back at my parent's one last time. They had resigned themselves to the fact that this was for the best. Being wise and spiritual, my mother knew that everything would be ok, and so did my father. When I

FREEDOM(E)

arrived at the jail, I had to go through the first of many processes to come. First the booking process, then bunk assignments. I was assigned to a quarter where there were a few familiar faces I noticed as I put my mat on the bunk and got settled in. The guy with whom I was most familiar was Johnathan. After I get settled in, I asked Johnathan for a pen and paper. I was going to write letters and more while doing my time.

My freedom(e) was centered in my field of thoughts. My "higher" thinking. I started "thinking" that I was an author and as you can see, I am! I knew I was a great writer. Although I was going through a rough time, I knew that I would only use this as a stepping stone to greater things. I dreamed of becoming a best-selling author and publisher and would be able to provide for my family. I knew that while I was incarcerated, I would be working on my dreams.

While I waited for the "chain" that would take us to the TDCJ (Texas Department of Criminal Justice), the prison, I read and wrote. They transported and interchanged inmates like they were trading stocks. It was like any other system. The school system gets funded based on the number of students, just as prisons did based on the number of inmates. Unfortunately, there was more funding for the prison system than for the education system.

I went through yet another booking and housing process. I was assigned to unit C-2. I walked in and grabbed the bunk at the back of the tank nearest the door. I put my few belongings away, including my writings and was ready to go about the process of getting settled in since this was going to be my home for the next 6 months.

We were identified by the wristbands we wore, and many guards busted our chops over this. There were mostly black brothers in my tank and only a couple of white guys. I asked a brother for a pen to continue writing on my dream. When I was writing it was a great escape. It was like this place didn't even exist.

After I'd been there for a few days a brother who goes by "Smooth" says to me "That's a long letter. You've been writing it since you came in."

I chuckled and told him it was not a letter it's a book.

"It's a book" he repeated mildly shocked. I

I told him yeah and began to read a few paragraphs out loud. He became so interested that he motioned for them to turn the volume down on the tv. Soon, my voice was the only thing that could be heard in the dorm which became silent as I read. All throughout the evening guys would come up and talk to me about what I'd read.

I wrote from the time I woke up until I couldn't stay awake anymore at nights. Some nights I would drift off and dreamed of being in other places, like South Padre Island. Sitting on a sandy beach with a good drink or smoking steaming African cannabis mambada.

I dreamed of my sister and I talking, laughing, and having the time of our lives. After each of my dreams, I was always disappointed when I opened my two eyes in prison and see how the choices I made in the past landed me here. Although this was a dark situation, I

FREEDOM(E)

knew that even in the darkest of dark my light was shining. I had to turn it around and make the best of the bad which I had. I opened my eyes to the inside of C-2 and I knew that while I was here, I would make a difference.

I didn't speak to my parents as often as I wanted to. The phone calls were so expensive, so I would only call if I was transferred to a new camp. I didn't want to give the prison system anymore of my money and at $5 for 10 minutes, I was going to sacrifice phone conversations. On that note my family knew why I didn't call often. One of the things I realized is that no matter what position I find myself in, I must be productive with my time. That's another example of freedom(e). The powerful thought process that helps you plan goals and stick to them. Freedom(e) to know you can accomplish anything if you stick with it. Outside interference from enemies and entities will leave you with nothing, including your dreams.

I had more than the usual amount of paper inmates were allowed in jail. Smooth looked at me and told me that I would probably have to mail the papers home if I wanted to keep them because they wouldn't allow me to have so much property catching the "chain" to prison. I didn't know if I had enough money or time to order a stamp from commissary. I had found out that the "chain" comes every two weeks and had come the day before I arrived. I figured I would have enough time to order the envelope.

I knew I had to exercise some faith and believe in myself. Believing in myself is a strong force that will lead others to believe in you and themselves. It's a great gift that keeps on giving. I was standing on faith that the commissary would come in time for me to mail my papers. My writings were very important to me.

I finished writing my last letter for the night, sealed it, and sat it on the ledge of the looking glass for the officer to pick up in the morning. As I laid in my bunk that night, I began to take deep, slow breaths. Meditating and concentrating on positive images and feelings. I drifted off into dreamland.

I dreamed of my youth and growing up with my cousins in our old apartments where our families lived. I dreamed of donuts and chocolate, eating as much as I want. I dream. I wake up. I'm still in my cell.

of the bottom bricks of 22 Lachmont Street. The bricks that made the steps up to the platform of the front lobby door. Opening the door and stepping through the threshold standing before the ground level land lord's apartment which wasn't so ground level in the first place. The door that leads to the two upstairs apartments my family's on the second. I grab my cousin and we head out the door, down the steps of the hallway and out the building heading for fields corner.

In my dreams I could eat as much chocolate and sweet and not feel sluggish. When we get to the fields I'm looking at Dunkin Donuts with that look in my eye like I'm coming for you. I wake up thinking of the dream and times with family all my cousins and what not. We may not always be at the same place at the same time. I keep family in my heart.

FREEDOM(E)

CHAPTER ELEVEN

FREEDOM(E)- A PHONE CALL. A LETTER.

Even as I write these words and think silently to myself, I experience freedom(e). The thought processes. Must I be placed in such a bad position before I realize my own worth? Will I end up with nothing before I finally appreciate my own value? I think not. I planned to make future choices that will land me in a position for advancement to greater positions.

I sat at the day room table observing the other inmates doing their best to pass the time. Some were playing dominoes and table games while others sat around telling war stories or watching TV. You also had a select few walking around, stretching their legs and exercising.

Commissary arrived, and I was able to purchase a large manila envelope to mail out my excess papers home in. I stuffed as many papers in as I could without it being confiscated and addressed the envelope. This is how I planned to send the pages to my book and other poetry writings. After sealing it, I placed the envelope on the ledge of the looking glass waiting for it to picked up in the a.m.

Once again bored, I went to my bunk and tried to escape into my dreams. I didn't understand how some of these guys could just watch TV all day or play board games or even stare at the same four walls all day every day. Our tank was small. It was an 8-man tank with very little room. I attempted to do a few stretches on my bunk to keep my muscles active. Shortly after, I closed my eyes to escape to freedom(e).

The dream I had this night was lit! In this dream I was teleported to Times Square. There was me and 2 other ladies, but I couldn't make out their faces. I saw myself approaching a vendor selling something on the sidewalk. As we walked up, my body felt light and a feeling of willingness seemed to overtake me. I realized I should be looking for something one of the ladies would like. I knew it was something that I would like to be the one to give to her. I wouldn't be expecting anything in return. I would only be happy if I could be the one to give it to her. It turned out to be her favorite flavor of gum balls. I searched an entire row for old school gumball dispensers. There were no flavors of this gum ball, so I searched another isle, then another and another. Just when I though there were no more machines for me search, a huge stadium-like thing appeared from thin air. The gumball machines were set up like they were seated on bleachers. I continued wondering if I could find the gumball. Since there were so many, I was afraid it would take too much time to search through them all. Aiming to please the young lady, I go past the first few machines and finally reach one that had the watermelon gumball. I reached down into the machine and felt the cold steel touch my hand. My feelings were strongly indicating that I would please her by finding it. Dreaming she would be pleased with me finding her favorite gumball, I hoped she would kiss the sweet taste of watermelon off my lips.

FREEDOM(E)

Suddenly the dream switched, and I found myself at the Broadway City Arcade. It was a cool place to have a good time and it wasn't far from my parent's home. I would go there often with my father, and although we never stayed long, we always had a great time. This time was different, only in my dream, I wasn't a child anymore. I wasn't in the mood to play games I wanted to bond with the young lady beside me. We bonded over the tones from the video games and the sound and the feel of the air blowing up through the holes in the air hockey table.

As I dreamed, I thought of how I hoped my life achievements would mirror the effort and perseverance I put into searching for the watermelon gumball for the lady. Some of my dreams were courting me. It seemed as if I was entangled in a ritualistic courtship dance. I was mad deep in thought!

I'm not sure what jarred me awake. When I realized it was only late evening, I wondered if it would be hard for me to sleep later that night. My brain always had to unwind from the sound of the TV that played in the background all day in this small space. A few knuckleheads didn't have the thought of appropriate sleep time. They drank coffee until late in the night and stayed up all night making sure no one else slept, laughing and giggling like a bunch of females.

I constantly had to readjust and readapt to the noise level of the tank depending on the day's activities before I was even subconsciously able to wind down for sleep.

I got up to eat and spent the rest of the evening reading. Surprisingly, I drifted off to sleep. Freedom(e). My dreams were peaceful that night. The dorm was so quiet that night, I felt as if I were listening to an old vinyl record with deep, sultry music playing to a deep beat. The sound of the music massaged my ear drums and catapulted me into another dimension.

I appeared standing next to my father. He was looking down at me and whispered, "We are truly home."

My soul vibrated with love and light as my father reached over and to pick up the needle on the record player that appeared. He lifted the wax record off the spinner and rubbed his fingers over the grooves. The music got me moving and my father smiled at me. I floated from the living room to the dining room a few times before going up the stairs.

I went into a room that was filled with records. Leafing through them, I found one whose cover caught my attention. I lifted it up taking a good long look at the album artwork. I took it with me out the room and shot down the stairs. I was running and jumping down all of them. It brought back memories of back in the day. I would oftentimes wake up the entire house!

In this dream, my father suddenly appeared in the same room I was in. To my surprise, my father places a record on the spinner and the song that played was from the same album I held in my hand. A warm feeling washed over me.

I woke up suddenly hearing my name being called loudly. They told me that I needed to pack up and roll out because I was catching the chain.

FREEDOM(E)

CHAPTER TWELVE
TRAFFICKING & TRADING

Because of my proactiveness, I had already gotten my things together, so when the chain came, all I had to do was throw all my county property into the mat, roll it up, and sit by the door. I said my goodbyes to all the fellows. When I got to Smooth, we both gave each other dap and he told me to keep writing my book. He was one of the only cool dudes in here, but I wasn't going to miss any of them.

I sat in the day room waiting for the guards to come and get me. Fifteen minutes later the guard walked In and unlocked the steel door and then motioned for me to come out with my things. We went back to the booking area where I was processed out and given the things I would take with me on the chain and the things I would send home.

After all this, I was transported back to the county to wait in a holding cell until they came with the chain to take us to prison. Sitting in the nasty cell reminded me how everything in the criminal justice system was designed to degrade you and humiliate you. I was startled out of thought by the sound of the steel door unlocking. I looked out the window and noticed a sheriff's van parked out front with an emblem I couldn't see from the window, but certainly not the usual county cars I was familiar with.

JASON MCMILLAN

They called my name and I was handcuffed by the sheriff who escorted me to his vehicle. He came back with a few more inmates and sat us in the van next to each other. Each of us had our bag of property that was placed inside a hatch in the back of the van.

The ride to prison seemed to be the longest transport I'd ever had. Being handcuffed in the back of the bumbling vehicle with no seatbelt on, seated to a bunch of hard heads didn't make it any better. I slept off and on during the drive. When we arrived at the prison, I was shocked. You could tell this was some kind of fucked up unit. There were big rusty watch towers and quadruple barbwire fences. There was not only barbwire on the bottom of the fence, there was barbwire all over the damned place!

When we pulled up to the sally port the driver and another officer get us all out and put us all in another holding cell for intake. On our way inside the building, I couldn't help but notice how beautiful it was outside.

One by one, we were called to do the initial part of the intake process. The entire process would take a month or so, so we were processed in sessions. We approached one of the guards who instructed us to lift our shoes to make sure we hadn't brought anything in She told us that we wouldn't be able to get anything past this point unless we had super powers. When she reached me, she looked at me sternly and asked if I had any super powers.

I told her, "Why yes I do."

"What's your super power?" She asked stopping in the middle of what she was doing.

FREEDOM(E)

"Making people smile!" I said brightly.

When she smiled at my answer, I told her, "See, they work!" Which made her laugh.

After the paper work they lined us up to cut our hair and give us our bedding and other necessities. All I could think of was hoping these six months would go by quickly. I sat and stared blankly at the wall waiting for them to come and send us to our next appointment. I was not actually staring at the wall. I was staring through it. I stared through at my future. I saw myself buying a new car and a house and talking on the Steve Harvey show, telling the world about my bestselling book: "Freedom(e).

At the three-week mark, we were at the final stages of the intake process. If you asked me, the process was way too long, but considering the number of inmates it held compared to the county jail, I guess it was understandable. Some of the last processes that decide where they house you is a medical checkup, IQ tests, and other educational assessments.

I was concerned yet excited about the educational assessments. I really wanted to see where I stood academically. Once I'd answered the first few questions, the answers began coming to me naturally. I was interested in knowing how well I'd done on the test, so when I completed the test I asked the teacher/guard when could I see the results? She told me that I needed to put in a request form and that they will give them to me. Because I was so curious, I went ahead and immediately filed out the form.

Eventually we were assigned a housing unit in the intake processing tank. I had been to jail a few times, but never to prison, so I wasn't familiar with all the rules. When I arrived at my tank and put my things away, I set off in search of the shower. I made my way through the rows of bunks and to the showers. Just as I was getting ready to jump in, an old school inmate tells me that if I got into the shower now, I would be written up. There were only specific times we could shower, and the time slots were posted on the wall. I tell old school "good looking out" and vowed I would get familiar with all the rules. Fuck getting write ups! I had an appointment for an exam and I didn't want to be musty, so I grabbed a towel and some soap and improvised.

Old School noticed I didn't have any deodorant, so he offered me some. I followed him to his bunk past the several rows of other bunks until we arrive at his bunk #28. He reached under his bunk and pulled out deodorant and baby powder. I used it quickly because of one of the number one prison rules: NO TRAFFICKING AND TRADING. This meant no loaning, lending, borrowing, trading, or bartering commissary or personal property. I used it quickly because I didn't want to get Old School in trouble. I thanked him for looking out for me and this began our first of conversations.

We were called one by one from the line of those of us waiting to see the doctor. Once I was examined the doctor told me that everything seemed to be good, including my lungs. I mentioned to the doctor that I'd had an extra nipple for years and wanted to know if he

FREEDOM(E)

could tell me what it was. The doctor explained that it was a skin tag. I called it an extra nipple because it hung from my left nipple although I hadn't been born with it. The doctor informed me that if I signed a permission paper I could get the skin tag removed. I signed the paperwork and removed my shirt to have the procedure done.

I started having second thoughts. I rarely took my shirt off because of the skin tag, not even in the summer unless I had a bandana to hang over my shoulder and cover it.

I decided to go ahead with it. The doctor shined the bright overhead light onto my chest and pulled out a long needle. The light hurt my eyes and I looked away as she injected me with the local antiesthetic. She picked up her surgical scissors and snip the skin tag. I didn't look, but I did hear it. Her assistant applied pressure while the doctor picked the tag off with her glove and discarded it.

It started bleeding a lot because it's a vascular area that got a lot of blood. She then tried holding a gauze pad to it, but that didn't work either. Then I heard a beep and a sound of pressurized air. I asked her what she was doing, and she told me she was going to slightly burn the area to stop the bleeding. She was becoming slightly frustrated because nothing she tried was working. She told her assistant she may need to get ready to stich it up. After giving me two stitches, I asked to see the tag. Pulling out the glove and opening it up, the tag looked way bigger than it did on my chest. I was happy though, now I could wear my shirt off in front of others without being self-conscious.

While waiting to be escorted, I have the blessing to have a moment of freedom(e), taking some time to think. Before all this happened, I had a car, a job, and an apartment. I thought I had all the things I needed which was true to a certain degree. This time when I got out, I'd have to rebuild and get all those things all over again. Especially a car. There weren't many places of employment within walking distance, so I knew that was priority. Due to my past actions, I fell short of my own expectations. My focus will be getting me out of the hole I dug myself into. I am looking forward to a bright, prosperous future with new business opportunities and successes. I am determined to go from mediocrity to greatness.

Freedom(e) is the freedom to think or choose how I feel, what I'm interested in and what I believe is most beneficial for me and my people. Freedom(e) to own your own business and be your own boss. Freedom(e) to choose to become an entrepreneur who established financial freedom by working on your dreams nonstop.

I had to learn this the hard way, but better late than never. I figured I needed a break from thinking so much, so I posted up with my cellie for a minute. Talking with the brother was cool. He had mad enthusiasm when he told stories from his past. He was mad smart too. He told me he ended up in jail for trying to cover up for a friend so that she wouldn't go to jail. He didn't realize that she had much more cocaine in her purse than he thought. He was given a couple of years for the crime, but he was so dope, he just didn't seem like the type of person to be here. There was a special

FREEDOM(E)

aura about him and from the looks of it, he felt the same aura from me.

Before long, I laid down to get rest for the night and escape into my dream land. On this night my dream landed me in a small space with stone walls and steel bars. What kind of fucked up dream was this? The steel bars were tall and reached up into a bridge-like arch. There were several people up there and some were familiar faces. I didn't care if they were familiar or not, I was feeling hot and I wasn't happy. The dream was getting intense as I chose to leave the stone building and save myself. Everyone in the dream seemed to be aware of my choice. I motioned for one familiar face to join me. He asked where I was going. I told him I was leaving. He shook his head no. I disappeared through the bars.

CHAPTER THIRTEEN
DESTROYING BAD HABITS

As I continued to do my time in the intake processing tank, I began thinking that maybe I was here to have freedom(e) from tobacco and other bad habits. Before coming to prison, with me being on the run, I had begun eating fast food and snacks from the corner store daily. I was starting to feel physically better now that I had three hots and a cot. It was sad that I had to become property of the state's prison system to eat regular meals.

Refocusing on to the positive thought patterns that had been growing since being here, I no longer wanted to have negative experiences be a part of my preferred learning method. I was determined to change that pattern having learned that the smartest way was not the hardest way.

My dreams were coming each night as different as they were frequent. One night I had a dream that I was young again and the only worry I had was if my shoes were tied. In the dream, I was riding a bike with another kid from my neighborhood. We were doing daredevil stunts and wheelies, seeing who could hold their wheelie the furthest. The dream switched and instead of riding bikes on Wyman Ave., I was walking through the neighborhood by the South Bay Plaza with my cousin Tyrone. There was a puppy walking beside us

FREEDOM(E)

and I remember feeling the sun on my skin and the feel of the gentle breeze. After a few blocks my cousin and I part ways. Each of us had our own paths so we hugged and dapped and he disappeared into the crowded intersection. I continued walking straight with the puppy. He was black with white spots. As I looked down admiring his cuteness, I noticed my shoes were untied. As I bent to tie them, the puppy licked my fingers. His tongue was cold and wet with saliva. It was so real I felt the wetness between my fingers and it woke me up.

I went about the normal routine of a boring day in prison. I was hoping to get a letter from my family that night. I hoped that my sister would at least take some time out to write me, but if not, I was sure either my father or mother would. I could expect something from them, even if it wasn't tonight.

There is no "one free phone call" in prison, so due to the fact of prison systems racked up money with extremely high phone rates, I hadn't spoken to my family since being here.

They did mail call and my name wasn't called. Not hearing from your loved one's while being incarcerated sucked, but I tried my best to keep an upbeat disposition.

This night it was especially loud. It seemed as if you could hear every single one of the 48 voices in the tank and if the two TVs were at their highest volumes. In this small space, the noise was constant and deafening. I sat around and shot the shit with a couple of inmates and headed off to dreamland.

My dreams had always been a part of my life. When I manifest in the dream world I know what freedom(e) feels like. Some dreams were so strong I wasn't sure if they were even dreams at all. Sometimes they felt like they happened and felt more like memories. I theorized the dreams were memories too.

The next day was as uneventful as the last. I did some numbers and if I figured everything correctly and not get in any trouble, my release date could be less than a month away. When you are incarcerated, the only think you have control over is your actions. I was in a process of recreation. When I get released my plan was to stay on a higher frequency above my old thinking and behavior until it becomes automatic.

Life had been trying to tell me something, and although I was just catching on, I was ready to listen. Even as I write these words, I want to encourage my readers to know that it's never too late to change. There will always be room for growth and improvement to do what it takes to make your dreams come true.

I was going to do what needed to be done so those who chose to witness my life would see a good example. An example on how things are done the right way. Freedom(e) to be great as I was born to be! As WE were born to be!

Freedom(e) to control my emotions, keep my peace, and to choose whom and how I love. Freedom(e) to choose the words I speak, things I want to learn about and things I want to understand. Some degrees of self-control had to be worked on and worked out like a muscle. Exercising it to build strength, flexibility, and

FREEDOM(E)

endurance. The same principles apply in building character attributes.

I had the Freedom(e) to make smarter/wiser choices in life; choices that will keep me going all in for the long haul and make my life's fruit as plentiful and bountiful as possible.

Another mail call and another evening of no mail. I wanted so badly to hear from my mother. My mother was the best woman in the world and I loved her wisdom and nurturing spirit. I will never be able to repay my mother for all she's done for me and I hope she will always know how much I appreciate her.

As I slip off into another night of dreaming, I anticipate a night of Freedom(e): a place, a state where dreams come true and nightmares don't exist unless you create them yourself. Freedom(e) was a quiet and peaceful place if that's what you desired, or busy and noisy if you prefer. A place where the space is vast and there are many great, wonderful places to visit. These places were places I'd been and experiences I had. These places and moments were Freedom(e).

In my dreams I experienced grant times and new places with family, friends, and strangers. The best dreams were the ones of and with my family. It was a blessing to be a part of a family like mine. In this dream, I was riding with my parents in their car. We turned on an unpaved, dirt road and motioned for my father to avoid a pothole in the middle of the street. He swerved, barely missing it. As we passed the pothole, I looked down to notice how extremely deep the hole was. It seemed to be a reminder to be aware of the road you are on in life to avoid hitting a pothole.

The ride felt therapeutic to me as we kept rolling down the road. We ended up at another relative's home and spent some time there. When I walked inside I saw familiar and new surroundings and felt a sense of comfort. The feeling went from one of warmth to one of terror. I began praying in the dream, not sure who or what I was praying for. As I headed towards the door, I heard someone call my name. I turned around and a strange woman asked where my sister was. I panicked as I searched for her frantically, suddenly, I hear someone say, "There she is!"

I turn to see my sister getting her hair done and I immediately wake up.

Damn! Waking up in this place was the last place I wanted to be. I woke up to find out the entire dorm had been placed on lockdown due to something that had happened on another unit. We go throughout the rest of the day on lockdown, but we were locked down before we were served our last meal for the evening. This was an example of a fool's harvest. The fool sows and everyone else reaps the foolishness.

I had learned to master my actions and reactions. I was close to my release date and I was not going to allow myself to be affected by the actions of someone else. Even with the lockdown, I was going to stay positive. I was starting to see the light and I wasn't going to be moved by reckless, loud mouth idiots who talked loud with their chests pumped out. They were doing their

FREEDOM(E)

best to portray hardened thugs for the sake of their egos. Again. Foolishness!

I had to admit, it hadn't been easy to make character changes for the better. It's hard to stop or curve the things I was used to doing. Over this year I had learned and gained strength so things that were foolish became clear and were spotted instantly.

I wondered how long the lockdown would last. I was extremely hungry, so I decided to try and fall back to sleep and escape into my own freedom(e). I must've fallen asleep for real, because my cellie was banging on my bunk waking me up for dinner. I jumped off my bunk and sat at our regular table for dinner. We were placed back on lockdown immediately after dinner and it was amazing to hear how quiet it was in the dayroom without the TV's blaring.

I was learning how to budget the money I had left with my family to send through my experience with commissary. It was ironic that I was this old and just now learning to budget, using commissary slips no less. I realized how much money I would have spent by now on tobacco products. If nothing else, the time here granted me a chance to regain my health and get rid of old habits.

I knew my parents had been praying up and down for me to quit smoking cigarettes. The time here would help me with that. I had a habit of smoking more when I was alone or depressed, but I planned on sticking with my new-found healthy lifestyle.

CHAPTER FOURTEEN
CHOICES

Instead of dwelling on the things I could have done differently I focused on the things I had to do and the things I had in my life that I was blessed with. Things like love and a loving family. Every day I opened my eyes was a gift. I had good sense for the most part and some genuine friends. Some friends as we grew older took different paths in life and we didn't hang out as we did in grade school days. Being in this unit sucked but it was nice to be around others.

I made a mental note of some of the positives of being incarcerated. One thing is how I had been living in my apartment for a year with no running water. Eating unhealthy fast food daily, I realized that since being incarcerated, I ate three square meals a day. With no running water I was unable to shower or use the toilet, here the showers and water utilities were always on. I was ready to release some sexual tension even now which reminded me of how reckless I had been. Perhaps this time detoured me from having unplanned children or even worse, an incurable STD. Children were cool, and I'd love to have some of my own someday, but not at the expense of a healthy relationship and a stable example of a father. That which is what I planned to be someday.

I also plan on finding that one young woman that would be the one special Queen in my life. When I've found

FREEDOM(E)

her, I will know because she will support my dreams and ambitions as I would hers. It would be me and her against the world.

The complaining from the inmates snapped me out of my thoughts. These knuckleheads continued to behave like ill-mannered children with no home training. They were sitting in this bitch like we were on vacation. Wonder how they would act when we got out of intake and got on a real cell block. This wasn't the county jail. There were people here doing big time and didn't mind fucking you up if you got out of line.

I began to get annoyed and tried hard to calm myself and my thoughts. Part of me wanted to bug out and bang on a few of these dudes, but I knew I would be sent to segregation locked down in solitary confinement. If I could have gotten away with beating one of their asses without the consequences of segregation or catching another criminal case, I would have.

That evening my name was called at mail call and immediately my mood lifted. I received a letter from my mother. Seeing her writing on the envelope made me smile brightly. With letter in hand, I walked through the day room to my bunk. I hopped on my bunk and opened the envelope that had been resealed by the mailroom.

I unfolded the papers and to my surprise, I see the first few pages of the book I had started writing in county jail. My people were on it and that felt great.

My mother wrote to tell me she was happy to hear from me and happy to know I was praying and of course she was praying for me also. I smiled knowing she was healthy and happy. I read that she and my father would be coming to visit me on my birthday. The letter was short and sweet, but I was excited to get the pages of my book and I was most-definitely looking forward to my birthday visit.

I was a little salty because commissary day came before I was able to buy stamps to write my mother back immediately. My freedom(e) allowed me to escape from old thinking patterns. Negativity was not a part of my genetic makeup. I was a naturally positive person. There was no way I could have doubtful thoughts with a spiritually centered soul. So, the negative thoughts I experienced were thoughts placed there by others. The ability to overpower negative thoughts, no matter how deeply entrenched, must be exercised. It is up to the individual to exercise freedom(e) and rise above the negativity and replace it with positive actions, thoughts, or situations. My letter from home was an example of the power of freedom(e).

We were finally awarded our "day room" privileges back. Yesterday half was restored, but today we have full access to the hot spot, TV, and we could move from one bunk to another. I was thankful I'd made it through the lockdown without incident. My worst fear was being gassed. I know it was juvenile thinking, but those were the things that could happen in a place like this. Three days of lockdown could drive anyone to escalate.

I used the power of Freedom(e) to escape the very essence of this place. Freedom(e) to rise as high as I choose. My vibrations were so high that negative vibrations could not survive in my presence.

FREEDOM(E)

Freedom(e) is exercising your choice to be free. Choosing not to be bound by your thoughts, especially the negative ones or choosing not to be bound by a corporate job. A lot of people who work in corporate America feel they have authority over the money they need to live and pay bills, but the way I see it, the authority they have is to make someone else rich while working behind their counters, at desks for their companies, and the authority to have you buy, trade, and sell for them. This is the same authority we must tap into to work for ourselves. You could build your own counter and stand behind it on your own authority. You could program your own systems and work them. You could be the authority to give others authority to buy, sell and trade for you. You must believe. Believe in yourself and believe in God.

I had discussed this thought with one of the guys in the tank. I was wasting my time because he couldn't or didn't want to grasp the concept of entrepreneurism, he stayed stuck on government thinking. His thoughts were that to make it, you had to work your way to be a supervisor in someone else's business. I explained to him again that jobs don't give money. Money is earned by work. His way of thinking was only his! It wasn't mine! This is my "job" and you are reading my "work!"

I didn't want to ever have to punch another man's clock. I strongly believed that and planned to follow my heart. It wasn't easy. Finished work doesn't fall from the sky. We must work hard to consistently reach our goals. Freedom(e) is opening your mind to the possibility of committing to hard work and expanding your character while being your own boss in the process. My goal was to open the hearts and minds of myself and others to the possibility of seeing that it can be done.

I couldn't wait to lay down and take off via my dreams. Pure Freedom(e). I couldn't wait to escape to another plane. I go freely, worry and carefree. I followed my soul, expecting to escape into my dream land, but for the first time in a long time, I slept peacefully.

FREEDOM(E)

CHAPTER FIFTEEN
SALE BLOCKS

About fifteen of us had gotten assigned to a block. Later we would be leaving the intake block and onto permanent housing. Niggas didn't know how to act on the intake block. The dudes who were always acting out were mad quiet today as we prepared to be housed with the "big boys."

I was laughing in the inside at all these dudes. They were quiet as mice. They had no idea what they were in store for. Neither was I. A lot of us were first timers to prison. We didn't realize that people really LIVED here. They went to work and school, had relationships, friendships, and drama. Nobody was going to be laughing or playing with these kids. That included me.

I reached underneath my bunk and got my things out of the bottom drawer. I didn't have much; just a red & white bag, a change of clothes, my papers, eating utensil, and a few hygiene products.

Later the guard came in and told us our housing assignment. They did a head count and escorted us down the hall, through doors, out the building, and onto the courtyard. They separated us by our individual housing assignments when we came to a gate that divided the units. I was the only one that had been assigned to unite F3C. Damn! I hoped it wasn't some fucked up unit.

JASON MCMILLAN

We were told to walk single file and on which side to walk on. There were four huge cell blocks that I could see out the window as we walked through the sally port. I noticed corny signs all over the walls when we entered the hallway to my unit. There was one poster talking about extortion not being allowed with a cartoon drawing of a body-builder-type guy holding a smaller guy in a headlock. I chuckled knowing I was in the big time now.

We walked around the sally port and the guys began to get out of line at their designated units. F3A, F3B, F3C… that was my cue to get out of line and get in where I fit in. When we entered the cell block, I head to my bunk and began placing my property in my new drawer. While I was doing that, my cellie got up from his bunk and stood in from of me rubbing his hands together like it was dinner time or either time to get something cracking.

Another dude from across the room raised up in his bunk and said, "Aye nigga, come here!"

I looked at him like he was crazy. He hadn't even sat up on his bunk and was talking shit about me coming over to him. Hell no. There was no way I was going to back down in front of all these people.

I barked back at him "ALRIGHTT HOLD UP LET ME PUT MY THINGS AWAY AND IN MY DRAWER AND IMA COME SEE YOU!"

The energy in the whole dorm changed. I looked back and my cellie was smiling and nodding his head like things were about to jump off. Everyone could feel it. Judging by the looks in the room, I could tell that no

FREEDOM(E)

one else had ever stood their ground with this dude. He was surprised too but it didn't stop him from getting up from his bunk. He wasn't new to this. I was.

I eyed him getting off his bunk. We stared at each other, but my look was strong and solid. I had a look on my face that said I didn't give a fuck about anything. He turned away and I went back to what I was doing. New block, new people. When I got my things settled, I went to the dude to see what was up. He told me his name was Dae-Dae and started welcoming me and told me where to sit. We were segregated by race, so blacks sat at certain tables.

I knew that if I had backed down initially, he and everyone else would know I was a weakling which would make me an easy target. He tried to bitch me and turn me into one of his minions by telling me who to fuck with or who not speak to. Then he had nerve to talk about my cellie. As soon as we finished talking, I went and did everything he told me not to do. I sat and talked with the duded he had beef with. If he thought I was going to be a bitch and take on his beef with these dudes, he was sadly mistaken.

Talking with my cellie, I figured he must have had beef with DaeDae over something stupid. Or he had probably stood his ground and it made DaeDae mad. DaeDae had a habit of trying to punk people. My cellie was mad cool but he ain't no bitch either. After that slick shit DaeDae tried on me I could see how he was coming and made it a point to be on my guard.

Eventually I got settled in. The first few days went by fast. Soon others were getting moved in and I wasn't the new dude anymore. One night, I wasn't tired enough to go to sleep, so I decided to exercise. Exercise not only kept me fit, it helped me to sleep. A guy two bunks down was trying to hold a conversation with me. I had nothing against him, but when I was doing my thing, I really wasn't trying to have a full conversation. He offered me a tea bag and I decline. Thanks, but no thanks.

A few days later we talked a little more. I didn't hold the conversation too long because of the way I felt about this place and the people in it. He offered me some hot chocolate. I accepted it, thanked him, then asked his name. He told me his name was Nick. Even though he seemed alright, I knew when people offered you a bunch of free stuff without even knowing your name, there was usually a motive behind it. Nick displayed selflessness towards me without knowing my name, so warning bells were ringing.

My cellie and I talked every day. Some days I fasted on speaking, but even when I fasted, he would still talk to me while I just listened and nodded my head. I had even written responses that he didn't mind reading. There were other guys, Walter and Brandon were mad cool too.

Nick's character was slowly being revealed. I sort of thought he was cool. For example, when you go to commissary in prison which is where inmates bought their hygiene, snacks, and writing material, it is an unspoken golden rule that your hygiene products come first. Even if all you have is money to buy those. There was a guy who went and bought all snacks then was

FREEDOM(E)

asking to borrow Q-Tips and soap. Nick wasn't like that. He was turning out to be alright.

That evening when dinner came, Nick was left without a tray because they miscounted and the only thing they had extra were diet trays. Diet trays were light and unfulfilling. Remembering the selflessness Nick showed me when I arrived. I had given one of the 2 pieces of cornbread I traded for something else. I repaid Nick without hesitation. Freedom(e) to be selfless and understanding that I don't need everything for myself.

CHAPTER SIXTEEN

CITY OF DREAMS

After dinner I laid on my bunk and dozed off and began to float freely into sleep. My dreams took me to a superstore. I noticed that I had a bunch of sweets in my pocket wrapped in brightly colored red, yellow, and orange wrappers. I knew that the sweets were not what I wanted, so I look around for a place to put them.

As I was searching for a place to put the candy, I noticed a stunningly beautiful young lady out the corner of my eye. I don't turn to look. She was so fine that I was sure every dude she passed stopped, stared, and tried to get with her. The last thing I wanted was to do what every other guy was doing.

I continue walking towards the sweets and place them all back on the shelf. There were so many rows of different types of candy, different colors, and flavors that I couldn't decide what to try next. My mouth watered seeing the chocolates and peanut butters.

I somehow broke free from my trance-like state and the young Goddess I saw earlier appeared right in front of me. We stared into each other's eyes, seeming to investigate each other's souls without fear of what was being seen or shown. I allowed my eyes to roam and take in all her beauty. I allowed my eyes to roam over her body. I noticed the royal blue sweater she wore with blue jeans and black boot. I was immediately attracted

FREEDOM(E)

to her and turned on by the thought of her. I began to fear she would see how she affected me, looking straight through me.

She looked at me with such an adoring look, to my surprise she was apparently fond of me. I liked it. I kept my composure, but it was difficult not to wrap her in my arms and kiss her madly. I kept cool and walked on through the store. Her head was visible through the rows of candy and I was shocked to realize that she was following me. I didn't mind at all, but I continued down the row knowing I couldn't get distracted but when I looked up, she was nowhere to be found. I saw a nice shirt and I knew that it would look good on me. I slipped my arms into the sleeves and stepped in front of a mirror. As I lifted my eyes to see my reflection I could also see the beautiful young Goddess. I turned to her hoping she didn't disappear like she did the last time. She was still there. I look into her eyes and smile, as she did with me.

I lifted my arms and she came to me. She laid her head on my shoulders and I brought her closer to me. I stared into her eyes like she was my heart's desire. It was apparent she felt the same way. Our lips join in a passionate kiss, our tongues intertwine as I taste the sweetness of her lips. We were caught up in a passionate embrace and I was ready to give her all of me. I thought that this was the romantic experience I'd ever had with a woman, which let me know I had been moving too fast with women in real life. I learned yet another lesson in this dream. Freedom(e) to be aware of what and how we act upon, what words we speak, whom and what we claim to love.

When I woke up and all I could think about was how beautiful and how pleasant it felt to be with her. It felt like I was floating on the vapors of the memory of the young Goddess as I took each step in the cell block. Sitting at the table waiting on breakfast to be served, all I could think of was the Goddess I experienced in my dream. I felt like I'd rather live life in my dream world.

I ate my breakfast and sat down to write a letter all the while thinking of my dream. All throughout the day I fantasized about being in beautiful places with this amazing Goddess. I dreamed of going through the canals of Venice, meeting with real estate agents as we shopped for homes and finally finding our dream house. I dreamed of having a daughter that was just as beautiful as her mother. I dreamed of experiencing domestic life, but one that was prosperous. Driving the latest range rover, living in the suburbs, and providing for my queen and princess would be like a dream come true. Dreaming of this Goddess has given me the motivation to want true and real love. Freedom(e).

FREEDOM(E)

CHAPTER SEVENTEEN

BOSTON & BROCKTON

I come from a stable family. Both my parents were good parental figures and although I got picked on my early years of school, I had fun as a child. Unfortunately, I was exposed to the wrong things at an early age. Things like sex and large amounts of money and drugs. I flipped my first bag of weed in the fifth grade and was placed on probation for other behavioral issues.

When I traveled with my family, I got a chance to see how other lived outside my neighborhood. One of the things that helped me not to succumb to thuggin' and gangbanging in the streets was that I started playing sports. I had a little brother who was killed to street violence. I found out that I was the intended target and my brother was killed instead. He was only 15-years old and I felt like I was responsible. The dudes that killed my brother shot through the window. Any of us or all of us could have been in the room at the time. I felt like I let my brother down being that I was one of the oldest of us brothers. In some ways, my actions seemed to always have a destructive domino effect.

Everyone from Brockton or Boston had one thing in common. We knew that the summers in Brocton are lit. Plenty of women, hustling, and driving luxury cars is what you usually saw. The summer my brother was killed was no different. One day, me, my two brother and two homies were walking down the street to go the meeting our gang held weekly in the hood. On our way, we had to pass an enemy gang's hangout spot. Thinking it was no big deal, we continued walking.

Just as we passed them, they started hollering and talking noise like they were about to jump us. We were ready. We were talking just as much shit. Since nobody stepped out the fence to start swinging, we kept it moving. As we crossed a block further up the street, we felt it was all good, but then see a jeep with dudes in the rival gang colors burning rubber up the next block. They had planned to cut us off and ambush us. We all saw them and knew what the plans were.

One of my homies yelled that we none of us were wrapped, meaning none of us had a gun so he takes off running and the others followed. I was never one for that running shit, so I kept walking while the other four ran. Before I knew it, they were up the street and out of sight. I was about to try and catch up with them, but I saw the rival gang's vehicle again and I wasn't sure if they were going to jump out.

I had made it right to the boys and girls club on my street when they caught up with me and jumped out. I had to philly cigars in one hand and an umbrella in the other. I dropped them and squared up, ready to fight these fools. I was never a super gangster but I damn sure carried myself like one.

Two of the guys ran up on me. One of them picked up my umbrella and swung it cutting my ear. I was squared up with the other two. I saw my homies at the corner of

FREEDOM(E)

the block and I was confused as to why they weren't coming to help me. They were looking at me and the looks on their face said they wanted me to get out of the fight safely, but they still wouldn't come help me. I noticed the look on my little brother's face. His look pleaded with me to stop so that no one (like him) would be killed.

I look around and see another dude coming from the jeep. He pushed the two guys I was squared up with and pointed a gun to my head. He pulled the trigger, and nothing happened. I look him dead in his eyes with his cheap ass gun. I look to my brothers and homies again. They were still standing there in shock.

The dude ducked down behind a stone corner of the building and pulled the trigger again. A shot rang out. If I would have been strapped, I would have laid all three of them out. The dude points the gun at me and closes his eyes. Nothing. He and his homeboys stood there like dummies looking down the barrel of the gun.

We were still on the Ave and in front of the boys and girls club which was a mad busy block. After standing there looking stupid they ran to get back into the jeep and burned rubber. I walked off to where my people were at to make sure they were alright. They were still in shock for a minute. Once we make sure everyone is good, we keep walking. That's what I meant by "I could have let it slide." Still I couldn't be sure they wouldn't come back. These fools tried to kill me. Do you really think I LET IT GO? Perhaps I could let it go if someone stepped on my kicks or something, but this fool squeezed three times.

Later that summer, around the fourth of July one of my brothers that was with me when they attempted to jump and kill me, drew up a map. The map detailed blocks and cuts and hang out spots for the rival gang. We even got a driver. We rode by their main hangout and just started emptying gun clips. After we shot the place up, we went to a safe house, then we all split up and went to different spots to lay low for a minute. After a while, I walked through the park. The Fall River JFK park was a beautiful spot. When I arrived back at the safe house, my homeboy "Shorty" told me that my father called. I called him back and he's told me my brothers been shot but he doesn't know which one or how it looks.

I got a ride as soon as I could. When I pulled up, I couldn't believe my eyes. The house was surrounded with yellow crime scene tape. There were no lights on in the house, yet I stood there knocking, not knowing what to do. Nobody was even answering their phones.

I felt horrible, I just knew my brother's being shot was my fault. The gang retaliated and hit my brother instead of me. I sat straight up in my bed, drenched in sweat. I must've fallen asleep again.

FREEDOM(E)

CHAPTER EIGHTEEN
EYES TO SEE

I was confused. How can someone say they are 100% sure they know the intentions of another. How can you be sure that the intentions and motives are pure and good, even when the person makes you feel uncomfortable. People are often blind to what they see and often ignore what they feel. The selfish, immoral, and unprincipled character some people have, often go unnoticed. This happened a lot with this new generation.

As I sat in the dayroom drinking coffee, I pondered these thoughts. I remember a story about a lady who ignored all the red flags and signs of her lover. She thought that since she'd met him at a Stop the Violence Rally, that she was being too critical, so she ignored the signs. Before long, she was in a full-fledge abusive relationship. She felt lost and wondered how it came to this. Truth be told, the guy did not have the emotional and mental capacity to give and accept a woman's love. On Valentine's day, the guy lied to her and told her he was meeting his mother for dinner, but only said that so she would leave, then he brought another girl over. After finding out he lied, she was devastated. It was a shame the guy couldn't be transparent enough to just be honest.

I have shocked myself on more than one occasion when dealing with the opposite sex. There is this one time I will never forget. I was in a relationship with a young lady at a time when I was trying to do things differently. My thoughts were on satisfying my heart and not my flesh.

My partner, however, was not on the same note. After 2 weeks of knowing each other, she was ready to have sex. I didn't want to jump into having sex "just like that." Don't get me wrong, I would have liked nothing more than to dick her down, but I wasn't ready to make the same foolish mistakes I had in all the other relationships where sex was the main attraction. I was transparent with her about the way I felt. Eventually, she moved on to find something different and I was cool with that. I always felt it was good to talk to your partner and be transparent about your feelings, so that there are no broken hearts or hurt feelings due to miscommunication or unrealistic expectations.

I was super excited about the visions and dreams I had. I dreamed of one day being a published author and living a beautiful life in Venice. I remember hearing that the African American writer James Baldwin was born on the East Coast but later moved to Italy during his career as a writer. I'd always heard that Venice was the Italian city of dreams. When I dream, I could feel the energy resonate through my body telling me not to ever give up and they told me that if I believed and did the work, I will achieve my goals.

My chakras were spinning even though I had to get them spinning myself. I had to reach inside and figuratively touch the wheels and turn them myself. I

FREEDOM(E)

didn't learn to do this overnight. It took me lots of time, practice, meditation, and faith. Those same characteristics were needed to continue to grow and flourish on my journey.

I had been working on finding spiritual and physical balance. My physical body seemed to want to be pleased with unhealthy food, relationships, etc. and my spiritual body wanted to be nourished. There were other parts of my character that were weighing me down. Pollutant thoughts of and feelings of fear, worry, and the most dangerous, hate. When I took control of these feelings it was easier to master the spiritual/physical balance. This to me was another example of Freedom(e).

I got up and went and sat on my bunk looking at one of my favorite shows on TV. On this show, they restore classic muscle cars. Watching the show took me back in time to the place where I had seen the show initially. I was at a homie's house from the neighborhood. I had stopped by to visit and when he invited me in, the car show that I was presently watching was on the TV. I became instantly enthralled.

The show fed my love for fast, hot rod cars. While watching the show, I began to relax and slip off into my dream-like state. I dreamed about all the cars on the show. I dreamed about the day I would have my own dream car. I knew I would have to work very hard, whether I worked fast food, day labor, or as a writer.

JASON MCMILLAN

CHAPTER NINETEEN
REBUILD

With every new day there was something new to learn and experience. My power of Freedom(e) was continually growing. I was diligently working to strengthen them. I focused on strengthening physically and spiritually. Best as I could in prison, I ate right so that I could carry the right amount of energy and vibrations. I made sure to get as much sunlight as I could which helped me to think clearer.

When I go to sleep and close my eyes and escape into my dream state, I am no longer bound by flesh, gravity, or matter. On this night after lights were out, I felt an instant pull into my world of Freedom(e). I dreamed that I was on my sister's couch. When it registered to my subconscious brain where I was, I was in disbelief. Then it settled in. I was getting used to teleportation, dematerializing, and materializing. I lifted my head from the cushions and stared directly at the entertainment center against the wall. I sat straight up. I could feel the place. I turned and saw my sister who was sitting on a chair against the wall.

I tried to say something to my sister, but for some reason in the dream, I couldn't speak out as I usually could. I had a question to ask her and although I could think of the question and even mouth the words, I could not hear a sound. I brainstormed and paced the room

FREEDOM(E)

trying to figure out how to audibly communicate with my sister. I finally figured that it wasn't meant for me to say anything to her. My dream state was illuminating the idea that my sister's spirit was not in a willing spirit. She was not willing to receive.

I woke up suddenly. This was the first time I awakened from a dream without a clear understanding. In the past, I wasn't open to new ideas. Since this thought process surfaced, I continued to keep my heart chakra open. Keeping an open mind to new concepts, ideas, and new results. Freedom(e). I am the creator!

I got up and walked towards the sinks to wash my face and brush my teeth. There were several guys up already. Some were drinking coffee; the others were sitting around reading or writing. It was surprisingly quiet.

I sat down to write and someone new came in the tank. He was quiet and off to himself. I went over to introduce myself. He told me his name was Danny. This was the last place I wanted to make friends, but this would probably be the closest I'd come to building a friendship with another inmate. Danny was Korean. He and I talked a lot. He told me a lot about his culture and his country and I shared with him about mine. I told him about my love for writing letting him know that I will one day soon be a best-selling author. He told me about his wife and their roller coaster, up-and-down love affair.

We were trading stories about our sisters and each of their accomplishments when the guard came in and told us to rack up for count. On my way to bunk to rack up,

I laughed to myself thinking about Danny and his stories. His sister sounded like she would be cool to hang with. I wouldn't mind getting to know a Korean girl.

We sat back at our table and waited on chow. While we sat, Danny continued the conversation by telling me about his career. He told me he was in the technology business, particularly cell phones. I shared with him my business plans and goals of being a property owner/investor, a best-selling author, and hopefully one day, a family man.

Danny told me his family owned a donut shop in the city I lived in. I thought that was a cool and interesting business to own. Danny and I traded contact information so that we can keep in touch on the outside. He told me that I should come to Dallas, Texas and visit sometime. I told him that one day I would come down for a three-day weekend. Truth was, I could see that a friendship with this Korean guy. Freedom(e) to build new friends and bridge cultures.

Danny went to his bunk to read while I sat at the table writing. As I sat there, another guy in the tank, Richard came up to me asking what I was doing. I told him as I had the others that I was writing a book. He asked what the book was about, and I explained to him that I was writing about my experiences; intermixing my life story with a new thought process. FREEDOM(E). He was taken aback by my concept. I felt good about that because Richard was a reader and his intelligence was obvious. He seemed very interested in my paradigm on dreaming and manifesting. The short conversation with Richard was short, but powerful. We ended the

FREEDOM(E)

conversation learning a little more about each other's future goals. I shared with him as I had with Danny mine.

As days went by, I started feeling better about life and even my current situation, because I knew I was getting better mentally, physically, and spiritually. I had full faith and belief in myself that my writing will take me far. I knew that one day my writing will provide for me. I will still incorporate a Plan B, C, or D if necessary.

One of the goals I set for myself is to become financially stable. An unstable financial foundation is rocky at best, but is not fit for a safe, strong, lasting future. I knew that I could never support a family in the future if I didn't get my finances together. So many people gave false images of support. Without financial stability, the only support I can provide is emotional, and some point, my Queen will want and deserve more.

With my goals and plans written down, along with supreme knowledge and wisdom, I know that I will make it. In my place of Freedom(e) there is Divine communication. This communication will give me a push or pull when needed. It will be a stress reliever and love at the same time. These feelings bring rejuvenation and a new meaning to the exciting feelings that unfold sensationally.

After our last meal of the evening, I laid in my bunk and read until I'd fallen asleep. Soon after breathing deeply for 10 minutes, I float on the wings of Freedom(e) into my dreams. In this dream it seemed as if I was tipsy. At one point in the dream I felt drunk which turned into feeling like I was drowning. I floated to the bottom of an invisible pool where I landed and stayed as still as a clam.

Suddenly the room filled with filing cabinets. The cabinets began opening and closing and the ground felt like quicksand. I felt a huge gravitational pull that threatened to swallow me. There was a mailbox that appeared. I could see someone walking to the mailbox and placing a letter inside. I reach out to them, motioning for them to help me, but the person turned their head and continued toward the mailbox. My spirit resonated with the thought that I needed to help myself out of the quicksand.

The filing cabinets started closing in, suffocating me and creating a feeling of pressure that began at the bottom of my feet up to my forehead. The pressure was excruciating, and I felt like my head was going to burst. Just when I thought I would burst, I rose up quickly as if I were in a horror movie.

I felt Freedom(e) within myself. There was a lesson to be learned. The beginning may seem uncertain, but you must be prepared to go to the end. Even the end there will be a new beginning point. Here was my Freedom(e). Freedom(e) to believe in myself, and you have the Freedom(e) to believe in yourself too! I knew my future held great things, experiences, and people. I won't fear greatness.

Suddenly, my dream switched again, and I ended up at a construction site. I remembered feeling that this land site was developed specifically for me. I looked down and saw tools and materials. Instinctively I knew that this was for the laying and producing of my foundation.

FREEDOM(E)

I looked down at the raw materials in awe. I could subconsciously feel myself getting out of myself and moving along, constructing effortlessly. I measured the twice, and cut once, making sure the frame work was done correctly. When I became confused or not sure of something, I would ascend higher into myself and ask the higher being in charge to show me how this goes, or to teach me to understand how this works.

I was answered and shown. I kept getting ahead of myself rushing back and forward from where the materials were back to the foundation I was laying. I started feeling frustrated and overwhelmed, feeling like I was going to run out of time. I started throwing things together which only made me more anxious. I asked the higher being once again for instructions and the ability to grasp and retain the information. I always received what I asked for. I discarded my lower self and continued to move forward toward and into my higher self, going back to build my desired foundation. Having received instruction gave me a great feeling of confidence. There was a feeling of assurance that ran through me and I knew that my foundation would be laid in the right way. Moving to the next stage of construction, I saw the foundation and the frame as if it were complete, before I had even started.

I was motivated and sure of myself. I was not ashamed to double check and ask for direction; something I hadn't been willing to do in the past. The old saying, 'Measure twice and cut once' had taken a new meaning. It was a great saying for a great purpose…. FREEDOM(E).

CHAPTER TWENTY

MOTHER FROM WHOM LOVE DELIGHTS

Even as I dreamed, I knew my foundation must be stable and secure. I had to make sure it was level before trying to build the structure, it would either topple over or collapse if it even stood at all.

Reaching this realization brought me to a place of peace which allowed me to go further and manifest my destiny. Breaking free, I found myself in a shopping center, talking to the "woman of my dreams." The Queen whom I tried to find special candy for. As I talked with her, I saw my mother walk in our direction. My Queen was nervous about meeting my mother. I could feel it, so I reached over and gave her a kiss and assured her that all was well. My mother approached with a welcoming smile. Immediately the tension evaporated. I could feel a sense of happiness as I could feel how proud my mother was of me.

This is what my mother has always desired, to see me happy, and to see my progress. She has always wanted to see me as the head of the foundation of a loving, happy family. Freedom(e) here it lies.

As I slipped deeper into sleep, I began tossing and turning. I was restless and irritable. I floated into a world full of vinyl records. The records were framed and hung on a wall. It was almost like I'd entered a huge music studio or radio station. I move through the

FREEDOM(E)

decorated halls again. I saw another beautiful young Goddess again. We teleport through to the next level where we relax in peace.

When we arrived at the next level, the lovely lady's appearance completely changed. I could see that she is at a higher conscious, and I am immediately attracted to it. She appeared to have a position of divine power and grace. I was naturally drawn to her.

I held my breath and lay completely still so that I could hear every word she said. Her lovely voice was like music to my ears. When it dawned on me that the words she spoke were my own, I became immediately aroused. Something told me that I couldn't stay long, so I prepared for departure. I was hoping to stay sleep longer, but the guards were calling out breakfast.

Later that evening, my name was called at mail call. I got a letter from my mother explaining that she'd lost my address and that was why it had taken so long for them to write. She went on to tell me about her daily activities, telling me about our family and their accomplishments, and the fact that they were still upkeeping and checking on my apartment frequently.

At the end of my mother's letter she stated that she would like for me to join along in studying the Bible with her. She wanted us to read and study the same book at the same time. I thought that was cool and that was something I was happy to do. Even with time and distance between we could both meditate on the same thing at the same time and we would still vibrate on the same frequency. My mother and I have a great relationship that we are always building and working on. I love it and her.

I thought about another dream I had the other night, although I can vaguely remember it. I once again left my body and went to another dimension.

In this dream I was at my Mother's establishment at Belmont Street. There was a woman out front of the shop sweeping that I didn't recognize. I went inside expecting to find my mother, instead I found the shop as it used to be years and years ago. The phone rung like a scene from The Matrix. My mother was on the end of the line. She spoke in code, but I understood it. She asked how long it would be before I could come and get her. I answered her back in the secret code language letting her know I wouldn't be long at all.

I took off out of the shop. Again, I saw the lady who was sweeping out front. She approached me and asked who I was and what did I want, trying to get information from me. I didn't give her any. Instead, I head out to my parent's home. As I got closer, it started raining. In my dream I could feel the comfort of the warm, soft drops. It felt so real that I wiped at my forehead which woke me up.

I sat up in the bed and took a moment to gain my bearings. After I had semi-awakened, I reflected on the dream. Again, there was a clearer meaning behind the dream. The lady sweeping outside the shop indeed represented my mother even though I didn't recognize her. Her sweeping represented how my mother took over the upkeep of my apartment. Me not finding her in the shop represented her being at my apartment

FREEDOM(E)

expecting me to be there. The speaking in code represented my mother missing me. I am sure every time my mother walked in the door of my apartment, she halfway expected me to be there. I was there in spirit. I am flesh of my mother's flesh. I will always be there with you.

CHAPTER TWENTY-ONE
KNOW THYSELF

The saying "Know thyself" resonated within my spirit. I believe to *know* thyself we must first *learn* ourselves. I was learning this through my life experiences and through my dreams; my life in a higher dimension. I believe that dreams are truly real life just as this one we live while awake. Only our "dream" life is not the one that we are used to, because we have no control over outcomes.

This is my belief. Energy cannot be created or destroyed, it goes from one form to another. When our physical life comes to an end that is when life as I know will end. Then I will go on to lead my life in Freedom(e). The one I have made for myself in the higher dimensions with the higher self and highest power. My real life may have started off a little rough and even a little confusing, but it will get better until I reach my point of greatness. I have seen it with my own eyes. My real eyes have realized the truth which has been reveled through revelation of dreams from the highest power in this world and the world I have manifested for myself and my dear loved ones.

On this day I received a letter. It was short and sweet. Her letter read that she hoped I was still expressing myself in positive ways that may be a universal benefit.

FREEDOM(E)

I laid my head down and closed my eyes and opened them in a new world. In this dream I was driving around town on my bicycle just as I did back in the day. Everything in my eyesight was illuminated. The glow symbolized how much I missed home. When I reached the block at Avenue D, I looked to the right and saw a full, yellow moon. The sight of the moon captivated me, and I couldn't turn my stare away from its beauty. As it sat there directly above the horizon, it provided the sky light, including the blanket of stars that encircled it. When I finally pulled myself away from staring at the moon, the dream switches and I cross over to another era of my childhood.

I see my mother and father arrive at Latchmont Street. There were several broken pieces of machinery and objects. We began placing all the broken pieces together and then testing to make sure everything was operating correctly and placed back in its proper place.

Instantly I am teleported inside my car riding down Columbia Avenue which dissipated into my bicycle again. I pedaled down the Ave to the 24-hour spot and saw my cousin standing at a nearby bus stop. We greeted each other, and he explained that he was headed to the south end. We headed in that direction together. I rode, and he walked. We were headed to Tyrone's. Although I knew the direction, my cousin took an alternate path. My surroundings were still familiar as we were still in my old hometown but as we came to a cross street, a Blue Pitbull puppy came out of now where and begun to follow us. He playfully barked, and it instantly put me in a good mood.

When we arrived at our destination, although I knew where this was in real life, in the dream, my surroundings were unfamiliar. We were headed to Tyrone's, but we ended up at a bank. This was an upscale, high class establishment. It was like traveling back in time to another dream, because out of nowhere the clear back pack appears. I walked into the lobby of the bank and was handed a prize for being a new customer. I sat down and admired my gift as I waited to be called by the banker.

Admiring the lavish décor and furnishings in the bank, my eyes spotted the RESTROOM sign. I walked to the restroom but instead of being toilets and sinks, there were men and women just standing around talking to each other. I felt like I had walked in the wrong place at the wrong time, so I turned around and sat back down and waited to be called.

I waited patiently and thought how I loved getting free gifts. The gift for being a new customer was a small token of appreciation that put a smile on my face. There was a lesson to be learned about myself in this moment. It didn't take much to please me. Something doesn't have to be new and expensive to put a smile on my face. Even if they were hand-me-downs. Knowing this feeling won't last forever, I was teleported to my Grandmother's house on Latchmont Street. All my cousins, uncles, aunts, brothers, and sister were there. I spend time with my family, but I knew that I had to leave.

I walked up the street and made a right at the corner headed towards the corner store. I noticed as I walked that each of the homes on the street had beautiful lawns

FREEDOM(E)

and fences. Some of the homes were surrounded in greenery and the others were covered in wildflowers. I loved walking through this neighborhood. I always had.

I walk into the corner store and asked the store clerk if he carried a specific item. He surprised me by saying, "Sure do Jason."

My head snapped up in shock. How did he know my name? Then I realized it was Mr. Chong. He had worked in the corner store since I was a little boy. After all these years from a small boy to a man, the corner store man still recognized me. He told me to check the next isle for what I was looking for. Shortly after turning the corner isle, I find myself standing at a beach to a fabulous body of water. Confused as to how the isle of the corner store turned into a sunny beach side, I sat and meditated. When I opened my eyes, I looked at the water and I could see living beings swimming close to the surface like the swim dancers do. They seem to be swimming in harmony with one another. Coming in together to form circles and then leave the formation simultaneously. It was very beautiful and breathtaking, and I knew that I would never forget this time and space. The beings looked to be human, but I really couldn't tell. They swam effortlessly like other life forms from the sea. Even though I was peaceful, I started feeling like it wasn't wise.

I tossed and turned in my bunk. My dream was switching back and forth so quickly that I was having a physical reaction. The dream switched again, and I saw myself in the car with my mother. We drove to her house and went inside. I sat on her couch. I think to myself as I always had, this was the most comfortable couch and place in the world. My mother handed me a universal remote. As I looked down at the remote, I felt a huge sense of responsibility towards me. This symbolized the smaller picture of the bigger picture of my life. I felt a knowing sense that I needed to reprogram the remote. I began asking the highest power for direction on how to bypass the process. In this instance I have only neural engrams and those had not fully come back to me. I pressed buttons like I knew what I was doing. It seemed to work, but for some reason I knew there were more steps I needed to take.

I felt the atmosphere thicken. I had to trust myself if I wanted everything to work properly. My higher self knew it was possible. I believed!

FREEDOM(E)

CHAPTER TWENTY-TWO
THE LIGHT

Just after my revelation that I needed to reprogram the remote, a new horizon came into view. I was in a battle with a force, a battle over my chakras and my kundalini. The weapon used was light. I knew I had an extra-special heart. My light source was true, and the others were false. This opposing force and false light was attempting to harm me, on the sneak to influence me so I that I would become attracted to the false light and digest its false codes. Those codes had the power to infect others just as it had the power to infect me.

This knowledge made me resist hard. I put all my effort, focus, and determination to overcome the negative forces that clashed and attempted to attack my progress with reprogramming the remote. They were attacking my righteousness. This negative force and I clash ferociously. My higher self was defending what and who I am, and this delusive force was looking to catch me off guard, hoping for my demise. Every tactic of attack it made I was right there to defend and counter. It was a very clandestine opposing force.

I swung my sword of light in every direction defending and attacking for the HIS namesake and for the sake of myself and for generations to come. Come they shall. After an intense fight I was back on the soft couch feeling complete.

My higher being opened my eyes to see myself reaching out to hand back the universal remote control to the creator; successfully reprogramed. That fact gives me a feeling of the oneness of the creator and me. I was thankful I completed the task at hand. In the third dimension, the left-brain world, some of the tasked asked of me to bring left brain results would not get completed. I may have fallen short more than a few times, but I always got back up! However, in this new dimension, my right brain would lead and control. I seemed to have become a sleeping genius. That was how I felt in the moment. I return to my lower-self humbly. When I awoke that day, I began to decipher more of my dream.

Today was my mother's birthday so yesterday I had a visit from my parents. My mother told me to ask her what she wanted for her birthday.

I take the bait and ask, "Mother, what would you like for your birthday?"

She told me what she wanted for her birthday was for me to be happy and successful. From that day to this day, I hoped to make that birthday wish come true.

It was a great visit. It was like old times with the three of us together. My mother told me about Prince's attempt to write me and even though he was my brother, all three letters were returned. I wondered if he was trying to send me something I couldn't have.

My father told me he'd went to the movies to see a new release and enjoyed himself saying mom didn't want to go with him. He went on to tell me that they went to the county jail to pick up my items, but they were too late.

FREEDOM(E)

The items were only held for so long before they are donated to other inmates being released. I was upset. My favorite jacket was gone. That sucked but I knew that I had to get over it or otherwise everything I was working towards was in jeopardy. I was working on detaching myself from material and worldly things. I knew when I was released none of the donated items would be as nice as the ones that I lost.

It was time to move forward and on to bigger things. Those types of things were replaceable. At this time, I knew my parents had a long drive ahead of them. They told me that they were going to enjoy the road trip as part of my mother's birthday weekend. They would be shopping, traveling, and spending quality time together.

After my visit I laid down to take a nap before lunch. I yawned several times and closed my eyes. When I opened them, I saw a grand stair case. It was a royal edifice and I stared at its grandeur in awe. I had begun to make my way up to the top of the staircase; step by step. Once I arrived at the last step at the height of the staircase I see a small hall way filled with bookshelves on both sides of me. I was flooded with happiness as I began to explore. I saw a desk by the left corner of what looks to be the end of the hall.

Upon closer examination I saw that there was more to this dimensionally than I once thought was a very small hall. I could also now see that the counter of the desk wrapped around the corner as well. I laid my eyes on more shelves full of books. I wondered how far, how high, the dimensions of space in this place. I saw a few other people appear who were looking and checking out some of the books. When a book was removed from the shelf a light takes its place. Other people were returning books, but none of them stayed long. Shortly thereafter, I found myself alone once again. I didn't mind. Peace and relaxation came through me like a wave of changing tides coming in and then moving out. I didn't stay too long before I was gone from this place and embarking on a new adventure. Wondering and looking forward to what was next.

I believe that everything happens for a reason and what's meant to be will be. If something doesn't happen-it wasn't meant to be. My life will go on exactly how it is supposed to go, and I will do exactly what I am supposed to do. I will not worry anymore of things to come, nor will I stress over things I cannot change. Those things already over and done with. I planned to be stress free and worry free for the rest of my life. I knew I had a great life ahead of me. I could feel it and see it, and sometimes I can even reach out and touch it.

FREEDOM(E)

CHAPTER TWENTY-THREE
THE RECORDS

I was in a deep sleep, dreaming peacefully. I dreamed I was in a place that was obviously near a stream. I could hear slow, resounding waves. As I turned around I was facing an apartment building of some type, maybe a college campus dorm. I stepped into a room that I instinctively knew was mine. There were others who shared the space. The apartment was spacious. It held a full-size kitchen, living room, and all the bedrooms were spacious.

I sat on the couch opposite the loveseat which sat in front of large bay windows with white curtains that seemed to float in the breeze. The curtains flew outside the window as the breeze seemed to pick up. The windows turned in to doors that led to a prestigious balcony with a wonderful view of the distant horizon.

Not long after I am not alone. I could see other entities. They were comforting and relaxing me. I suddenly remembered I had something in the refrigerator that I had a craving for, so I snapped out of the daze and opened the fridge. When I did, a feeling of enlightenment washed over me as if just looking in the refrigerator filled me up with all the nourishment I needed. After this I became lackadaisical, slowly moving towards the balcony. I wasn't sure if the entities had anything to do with the negative vibrations I was feeling. I didn't know why. I didn't think I was doing anything wrong, but I was obviously conducting myself in a manner that was unorthodox from what they were used to in their paradigm of life.

I received these vibrations from others often being that I am an extremely right brained being, so various solutions come to me very naturally. The entities all wondered what it is that I was doing, and I wondered why they couldn't clearly see what I was doing right before their eyes.

The dreams I had transcended through the walls and steel doors, past all the locked gates and quadruple barb wired fences and watch towers. They carried me far away from anything or anyone egotistical, ignorant, arrogant or superficial. My place, my new place was away from everything I'd known before. A place of new things, new spirit and new life. Away from everybody who thought they knew me, but never actually took the time to get know me or even get to know themselves for that matter. My dreams carried me away from the pressure of doing things I knew weren't right just to be considered "cool" or having things like money, so it appeared we were "cool."

Despite my position at the time I must say I had made it a long way, and things could have been worse. I've come far from a fucked-up state of thinking and from some of my past actions that have caused chain reactions those same actions that once led to my young innocent brother being untimely killed. I knew I had influenced more of my brothers to dust off their shoulders and not over react to confrontation, but rather be proactive, so as not to be dragged down by another's

FREEDOM(E)

negative actions. I will always help to influence my brothers to keep them out and away from this place I am in now. Locked down physically, emotionally, and spiritually.

I knew that once I leave this place I must stay out. It was a miracle that I'd gotten as short of a sentence as I had. With everything I'd learned about myself and my life, this time had been a miracle. It taught me to detach. Fighting my cases and working to be financially ready to do time prepared me for this moment. This experience enriched my knowledge and wisdom.

I knew my time in prison was coming to an end. The days were longer, but the nights were fantastic. I could always slip off into the abyss of my dreams. On this night, I was teleported to my childhood home in the room I grew up. I stood in front of my dresser in peaceful silence, then reached into a drawer and pulled it out. I saw a few of my father's vinyl records inside. My record player that I'd gotten from my parent's for Christmas sat on top of the dresser.

I retrieved one of the albums. It was the trifold Motown Collection. I grabbed a single record, swung the needle's arm to the side, and placed it on the turntable. I heard a slight scratch as I placed the needle between the grooves of the record. I heard the most pleasant sound as the record spun. It wasn't a melody, instead it was the beautiful voice of my mother which sounded like music to my ears. Her voice spoke to me, encouraging and reassuring me that I was on the right path. It pleased and warmed my heart and complimented the feeling of being in my childhood home surrounded by memories.

I stood still and listened for a moment. I became so
filled with bliss and enthusiasm to the point it began to
flow from me in a translucent energy. Not only that, it
began to run through the house from out of the room,
down the stairs to my parents' room. The energy was in
search of my mother who was nowhere to be found.
When I realized that she was not there my soul slightly
declined in the moment of excitement. I could only
hope she will answer the call of her son. I woke up and
yawned, looking around the prison cell knowing she
would.

FREEDOM(E)

CHAPTER TWENTY-FOUR
BRANDON KNOWS KNOWLEDGE

Every weekend for months I sat down to help one of the
inmates, Brandon, out with his reading. He was at the
beginner's level and was going to classes at the jail, but
he wanted to learn more on his own. When he asked if I
wouldn't mind reading with him on weekends, I felt
honored. Of course, I would. One Saturday after the last
meal, Brandon came and sat on my bunk to read.
Usually we would each read one story from a book of
many short stories. This time, we each read three stories
apiece. Brandon was getting much better with his
reading. I was glad to be able to help. Brandon asked if
he'd shown me his report card, when I told him he
hadn't, he jumped up to go get it. His report card
showed he had improved tremendously, 3 times as
better than when he first began.

One of the new guys asked if I was helping Brandon to
learn to read and sound out words. I nodded my head
yes and he patted me on the back, telling me I was a
good man. That meant a lot to me that the others could
see my character radiating from within me.

Last night I had a few visions. The first dream was
initially still and silent. Although it started off quietly, a
convoy on a lone highway, I saw jeeps and hummers.
We were in the middle of nowhere. This couldn't
possibly be our destination. It seemed to be the middle

of nowhere, even though everywhere is somewhere. I believe I recognized this place, and it's not far from my home. This road leads to a place where a temporary job was waiting for me until my career calls. I spoke to my higher self and explained that I knew where this road leads. Next, I teleported to another road that I knew of. On this road I see dumpster trucks lifting to empty dumpsters full of garbage. This was good. It was a sign of my body getting rid of all the unnecessary garbage and pollutants. I woke up and my left eyelid was swollen. I wish the trucks had taken away everything that caused my eyes to swell as well.

Last night, the new guy Nick and I were engaged in conversation. He was first telling me about a man he knew that crossed the border illegally who began working a construction job to provide for his family. The same man bought a home for his family and began to work on the house himself! After it was all fixed up the man sold the home for double what he had spent to buy and repair it, then bought another home and did the same thing again. Now this man became very rich and earned his citizenship so that he was no longer an illegal. This story was a great inspiration. Then Nick started talking to me about God. I was cool with that. He asked me if I believed in God and if I believed that he sent his son to die for us? I told him that I would have to say yes although I don't claim a religion, I was still very spiritual. Nick told me that he understood and explained that God loved us and wanted a loving relationship with us. Nick asked if he could help me help Brandon with his reading on weekends.

FREEDOM(E)

I told him that if Brandon didn't mind, neither did I. Nick told me that it was rare to find someone in prison who had that kind of patience with others. He told me he could see my heart by my actions. I was glad that I didn't hide my heart nor let it hinder my actions. The actions were me. The real me.

That night, I had a very special soul ride on my royal road. I saw a place that looked to be where my homeboy Jamal's family house was on the top of the hill. Only now the house was my own. I was in my two-car garage. I have company. I sensed they were my family and friends, or they may be the forces within me. They were on the left and right. There was something I started that I was trying to complete. I was getting slightly frustrated because the mistakes I was making, I couldn't seem to control.

The forces were opposing each other. One force within me only seemed to care for itself. The other force sought diligently for understanding and to understand more. They both listened to the song of my soul and do their best to comfort me.

When I woke up, I thought about the dream I had and what it meant. I came into revelation of the fact that it helps get through the pain of life when someone offers to listen or to help in any way. When someone offers up any part of their life to make another person feel comfortable, that is the true meaning of sacrifice. I've sacrificed for people and others have done the same for me. It has meant a lot to me and would never be forgotten.

Reading and writing was a way to flee from this place. I wasn't trying to escape completely. I needed to remember this experience, because if I suppressed it like the others, I would never learn the lessons I needed to gain from this experience. For this reason, I tried my best to stay grounded. Whenever I wasn't sleeping and escaping off to my world of Freedom(e), I was fully grounded in the moment.

It seemed as if time flew by and I looked up and was 26 years old. It seemed just like yesterday I was in elementary school. Before I'd started school, my sister would teach me to read and my mother would teach me to write in the back of my mother's shop.

I wanted to be free from this place and free from this disgusting memory, but I needed the lesson to help other friends or family who may be traveling down the wrong road. The memories will be forgotten, but the lessons won't.

FREEDOM(E)

CHAPTER TWENTY-FIVE
I AM THE CREATOR

Instead of looking back, I intended to look forward towards my great future. I dreamed and planned where I'd like to see myself in life in 5 years, then again in 10. I believed that now that I have learned the art of manifesting my destiny, my reality at the 5 and 10-year marks will merge.

I had made a few acquaintances while being incarcerated, although that was never my intention to make friends. Despite my reservations about friends, there were a couple I considered friends, but my main friend was my cellie Lee. We had gotten close over the year. We talked and worked out together. We also ate our meals together. That was what sparked our friendship. He invited me to eat with him when I, myself was new. This selfless act in a place as hardened as this created a very strong bond.

As I was sitting at the table writing a letter, Lee came up and told me how good of an investment the earplugs on commissary are. He told me that the new earplugs in stock could block out just about anything. Just then one of the men in the tank screamed at the TV show he was watching, Lee told me that it would block everything but him, pointing to the man. We both laughed.

A few days later, Lee surprised me with a brand-new pair of earplugs. I thanked him and then put them in to try them out. They work excellent. I used them at various times during the day that day. I didn't want to wear them out. I decided I would only use them when the noise became unbearable.

Later that day and incident occurred, and we were placed on lockdown. For that moment it was quiet since no one could watch TV or use hotpots. It was quiet until the Sergeant walked in. The men escalated, asking when we'd be off lockdown. He told us that if we kissed the night shift's ass, then they would be nice and take us off. As soon as shifts changed, we were taken off lockdown. I immediately reached for my new earplugs and they worked like a gem. They muted all the nonsense so that I could finally fall asleep. I'd gotten there fast, drifting off to my place of meditative structure.

In this dream, I was riding on the passenger side of my sister's Mustang. We rode along the highway for some time. After cruising along for a while, we come to a turn, but as we approach it, the car seemed to lose control and I feared that we would crash and burn. I closed my eyes in fear.

When I opened them, I was relieved that we were safe, though we were no longer on the highway. We ended up on a different road. I looked all around in disbelief. I suddenly feel my parent's presence, then I see them. They came up from behind my sister driving different vehicles. Then they passed us, so we followed. We arrived at our destination which was a restaurant. After purchasing food from the front counter, I spotted the

FREEDOM(E)

end table from my parent's living room, the same one they had by the window when our family shared an apartment. I was instantly drawn to it, wondering what it was doing in this setting. My father was trying to tell me something. It was breaking my concentration. I was trying hard to go back to original task when I was physically awakened by the laundry crew.

Damn! Back in prison. The laundry crew was making their morning rounds and then breakfast would be served shortly after. I stretched and said good morning to Lee who was up reading his Bible. After he finished, he asked me how I slept. I began telling Lee about my dream life and about the dream I'd had the previous night. It must have triggered his neurons because as soon as I told him about my dream, he told me he'd had a similar one the very same night. The only difference, his dream involved me.

He told me that in his dream we were at the top of a huge canyon. The part of the canyon where we stood had a faulty rail that was unstable. Le and I were painting rocks on the canyon. There was also one other acquaintance of both ours with us, though he couldn't remember who. He told me that when I looked over the edge of canyon, the railing wobbled, and our acquaintance jumped over it. At the same time, a boat was passing in the water underneath the canyon. When the acquaintance jumped onto the boat, it lost control and crashed into the wall of the canyon. The boat began to fill with water and snakes and by this time Lee had fallen into the boat as well. He screamed for me to reach down and help him because he couldn't swim. He told me that I reached down and pulled him out and rescued him from drowning. He told me that the dream was so real that he woke up gasping for air.

I thought for a bit about his dream. It was a great honor to be the one who rescued and saved someone, but ironically, I can't swim. His dream probably meant something different to him than it did to me. Different images represent different things individually to each person, this is one of the paradigms of life.

After speaking with Lee, I went on about my day reading over the things I had written since being incarcerated.

Freedom(e) from this place meant freedom from policing to me. Freedom(e) from imbecilic activity. Freedom(e) from being drawn into others' negativity. Freedom(e) from returning to be a low-vibrational, root-chakra-stuck, being. There were many of those types right in this place. I was free from doing what most of the inmates here did to pass the time. They considered prison and the war stories and race wars entertainment. I was set apart because I had thoughts and a heart of my own. I am a man of my own. I passed a lot of my free time writing. This was one of the many things I did to pass my time and writing a book that would secure my future was what I considered entertainment.

FREEDOM(E)

CHAPTER TWENTY-SIX

DECISIONS

We all have decisions to make. Some of them will bring good and great rewards and others may cost us our livelihood or even our lives. I vowed to be conscious of my decisions from here on out so that could reach my destination of goals as I had dreamed of so vividly.

I pulled out the last letter I received from my mother. She had included old photographs of happier times. Gazing at family photos taken from our last family vacation, I go freely back to those moments of happy feelings; sunlight, the beach, palm trees, and most importantly, my loving family.

Last night I'd had a strong dream that aroused my emotions concerning one of my brothers. In my dream, something had happened at his place of employment, and I found out about it telepathically. I went to meet with him at a huge grand theatre. This theatre so dominating, it was 10 times bigger than the Strand Theatre in Boston.

I entered the theatre with other people behind me. On the stage sat my brother at a grand piano. I called out to him before walking up and say to him, "You are attempting to do right, and they retaliated against you because of that."

He didn't say anything in response, instead he began playing the piano and singing a song so beautiful that it made me cry. Buried memories begun to surface; memories I thought I'd forgotten about. Near the end of the song, we transcend to a different place. I was smoking a cigar and traveling on words and notes of my brother's song. When the song came to an end, I found myself being teleported to a park where I sat on a bench. A young lady comes out of the darkness and sat beside me. My dreams merged into multiple visions. I found myself standing outside of a home goods store. It was the biggest store in the shopping plaza. Near where I stood on the side walk, there was a small pond directly across the street.

I saw a beautiful water fowl swimming fast, zigzagging through the water and then another came following close behind. Whatever the first bird did so did the second one, flying in the same zig zag pattern. When the first bird stopped and put its head under water and so did the second. I looked on in amazement. Next thing I knew the birds came up out the water and started heading towards me. I thought nothing of it at first, but then they got closer and started trying to peck at my ankles with their bills. I tried to get away, but they began to pick up speed along with me. So, I ran faster and faster until I created some distance and got away from these crazy, ankle-pecking birds.

In yet another dream there were also birds involved, and like before, one was chasing and mimicking the other. The birds were black with a red stripe starting from the tops of their heads and running down their backs. They were all over the roof of a building. One

FREEDOM(E)

ran while the other gave chase. Wherever the first one would go, the second would follow. There was no specific pattern that this bird made, but I am glad these birds seemed to be on another level and were not concerned with pecking my ankles.

As I pondered over the dreams the next morning, I thought how I'd always had a hard time falling to sleep and staying asleep. This was my year of rehabilitation. Since experiencing Freedom(e), I had no trouble going to sleep anymore. This was a sign of all the stress that had been lifted.

I had been gradually taking steps to make the necessary changes that began here but would last throughout the years.

Another weekend came and went. I had finished reading with Brandon and was complimenting him on all the progress he'd made. I was getting ready to leave and get out soon, and I would miss reading with him. We had a few more books to read by next weekend before my release. The final books would represent the beginning of a new chapter for both of us. I felt a great deal of fulfillment helping Brandon learn to read.

Throughout that week, I seemed to have had a myriad of dreams, a mixtape of them! I was having dreams about my future success; how it will look, and what temptations it will bring. Furthermore, how I will deal with them. I knew that I will deal with them well. I dreamed of the things I will invest in. First myself, next my state of independence in many different aspects. In every aspect I will invest in myself and one day a family of my own which will ultimately be the best investment ever! I dreamed of owning a business that provided jobs for ex-felons and underserved people.

Finding new inspiration through meditation, I meditated daily and started doing yoga. I had no fear of falling or failing because I know now that I can fly. I can fly away from this place and any other negative situation in my life. When I am released to go home, I will bounce back and move forward and onto a great life. I will rise early in the morning just before the sun rises above the horizon. I will find a nice place where I can see the sun and dig into the earth a small hole to plant my feet. I will meditate with my feet planted in our mother earth; relaxing and focusing. I will do whatever I am comfortable with and may likely go past my comfort zone.

I envisioned myself in a great position ten years from now with my desires I've always dreamt of being fulfilled, while setting and aiming for new ones for the next ten years. I brainstormed daily, raining down ideas and options on how to be successful. I picked just a few at first and then came up with a plan that would increase myself and my wealth with every step.

I knew these steps must be taken to get to where I would like to be and eventually stand firm. Sometimes envisioning the future ten years from now does get cloudy, but then I think to myself ten years ago I didn't plan on being where I am now, either. So, with that in mind, I continued to plan.

We sat around talking about the lunar eclipse that was supposed to take place that night. We'd heard about it on the news. Because of our choices, neither of us

FREEDOM(E)

would get to experience it this year, but next year I planned to open the front door of my own place to step out and watch it. This helped me to maintain a positive demeanor.

They did mail call at 9:45 that evening. I didn't get mail, so I went to my bunk to see if I could see outside at the moon. My bunk had a window next to it on both sides. Although the windows were clouded with shoe paint, enough had evaporated over the years that I could see the moon if I squinted. I still didn't get to catch the eclipse. The position of the moon had changed and so had my own position. It changed from consciousness to subconscious as I drifted off to sleep. Sleep was one of the biggest human freedoms that could not be taken, only surrendered.

In this dream, I'd taken another trip down my royal road. It was my birthday and my family and friends were with me at my parent's home. I stood in the kitchen gazing at all my guests. I walked through the dining area and spoke to each person one at a time. I felt a sense of welcome and of unconditional love so deep, that it took my breath away. I woke up inhaling through my nose deeply. The day of my release had finally come.

Of course, this morning felt different. I could feel the day's potential and the potential of days to come raining down success on my skin. After I ate breakfast, I didn't waste any time packing my things and getting organized to go. I had already said my goodbyes the night before to the dudes I had built connections with and at 10 am, the guard walked in and announced my name.

JASON MCMILLAN

The guard walked me to the same cage that I was placed in when I first got here along with the three other men to be released today too. One by one, each of them were released to their loved ones. I was the last in the tank. The admin lady came and handed me a shirt and pair of jeans through the gate. I got dressed in them. The jeans were mad tight, but they'd have to do.

A man in regular clothing walked in and spoke with the deputy clerk at the counter and they call me up and ask where I lived. I gave them my complete address and she wrote a voucher so that I could have a bus ride home. She handed the voucher as well as the other paperwork to the man who then handcuffed me and took me through the building and out the front. It felt good to be headed home.

We arrived at a white van and the man unhandcuffed me, then opened the door for me to jump in the back. He got into the driver's seat, buckled up, and proceeded to drive down the street.

I looked through the windshield admiring the grass and the trees. The sunshine was brilliant, and the sky was bluer than blue.

The officer looked back at me and asked was I ever coming back to prison?

I gave him a crazy look and said, "Hell no, I'm not coming back nor looking back!"

About twenty minutes of driving, we pulled up to the bus station. He came around and opened the door, handed me my paperwork, and let me out of the vehicle.

FREEDOM(E)

"Good luck," he said as I walked away.

I didn't believe in luck. Luck has nothing to do with divine intervention.

It felt great to be out of that hell hole. After exchanging my voucher for the appropriate bus tickets at the ticket counter, I went to find a restroom. It was good to finally have privacy, but the stall felt extra small.

I washed my hands and found a seat in the lobby to wait on my bus. Looking around in awe, it was still hard to believe I was out. Now that my body was free I must keep my thoughts free as well. I will be sure not to get caught up in any destructive habits or vices.

After about an hour and a half the bus arrived and passengers started loading in. I was so excited to get home to my family. The bus ride was super relaxing. I loved to travel so it was therapeutic to me. Looking out the big bus windows at the clouds and all the open grass, I felt a peaceful excitement that almost overwhelmed me the closer we got to the station in my city.

As I made my way to the front of the front of the bus, walking in line behind the other passengers, I see my parents waiting outside for me. When I stepped down the ramp, their faces light up at the sight of me. I ran to them and gave them each a big hug. We were all smiles at we walked to the car. My mother reached in her pocket, surprising me with a pack of chocolate covered graham crackers. She knew those were my favorite.

It felt good to be in the comfort of my parent's care. I smiled with knowledge that Freedom(e) was here and it was time for me to apply my plan. It was time for me to be my own boss and become a published author. It was time to do the work and not only expect my results but manifest them. With all the work I'd done since being locked down, I knew that the only person who could stop me was myself. I would not allow that to happen. I will continue to keep working to see what the universe has in store for me. From what I could tell so far, I had a good idea.

FREEDOM(E).

FREEDOM(E)

ABOUT THE AUTHOR

Jason McMillan was born in Massachusetts, raised in the cities of Boston & Brockton. As an inner-city youth, Jason had early childhood issues, including being on juvenile probation at the age of 10. He moved to Texas after his freshman year in high school and ended up doing time in prison.

Jason McMillan is an avid reader and writer and currently resides in Central Texas where he pursues working for himself in various community-centered projects and is also a Performance Poet.
For years Jason considered himself to be an Urban outcast, but today thanks to the power of Freedom(e), Jason is well on his way to leading himself and others to a more spiritually conscious way of thinking.

JASON MCMILLAN

ACKNOWLEDGEMENTS

I would have to thank my Mother and Father for being strong, stable parents and sticking together to show me the way, and for the love and support.

A special thanks to my publisher TiTi Ladette for believing in me and working with me through her busy schedule.

Thanks to all my family and close friends who believed and encouraged me and anyone else who encouraged me along the way.

A special thanks to the Sigma Theta Sorority Killeen chapter for hosting the 2017 Literary Festival and to Dee Jones.

I thank the people who laid down examples before me such as all the Published authors I've met along the way, role models, and business men & women.

Thank you all again for setting examples.

Made in the USA
Middletown, DE
13 July 2019